T-34
vs
StuG III
Finland 1944

STEVEN J. ZALOGA

OSPREY PUBLISHING
Bloomsbury Publishing Plc

Kemp House, Chawley Park, Cumnor Hill, Oxford OX2 9PH, UK
29 Earlsfort Terrace, Dublin 2, Ireland
1385 Broadway, 5th Floor, New York, NY 10018, USA
Email: info@ospreypublishing.com
www.ospreypublishing.com

OSPREY is a trademark of Osprey Publishing Ltd

First published in Great Britain in 2019

A catalogue record for this book is available from the British Library.

Print ISBN: 978 1 4728 3235 1
ePub: 978 1 4728 3236 8
ePDF: 978 1 4728 3234 4
XML: 978 1 4728 3237 5

Maps by www.bounford.com
Index by Rob Munro
Typeset by PDQ Digital Media Solutions, Bungay, UK
Printed and bound in India by Replika Press Private Ltd.

22 23 24 25 26   10 9 8 7 6 5 4 3 2

The Woodland Trust
Osprey Publishing supports the Woodland Trust, the UK's leading woodland conservation charity.

www.ospreypublishing.com
To find out more about our authors and books visit our website. Here you will find extracts, author interviews, details of forthcoming events and the option to sign-up for our newsletter.

Author's note
The author would especially like to thank Esa Muikku for his extensive help on this book. Thanks also go to Andrey Aksenov and Yuri Pasholok. Place names in Karelia in this book generally begin with the Finnish, with the contemporary Russian version identified on the first occurrence. Unless otherwise noted, all photographs are from the author's collection.

Title-page: A commander's cupola, as shown here, was finally added to the T-34 Gaika turret starting in the autumn of 1943. This T-34 Model 1943 of the 222nd Separate Tank Regiment was knocked out by a hit against the driver's hatch during the fighting near Vuosalmi (now Druzhnoye) in the summer of 1944. (SA-kuva)

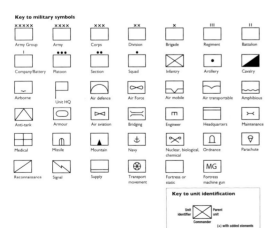

CONTENTS

INTRODUCTION

The T-34 medium tank is the best-known Soviet tank of World War II. A revolutionary step forward in tank design when it made its combat debut in the summer of 1941, it went on to become the backbone of the Red Army's tank force, and was manufactured in larger numbers than any other tank of World War II. (The early development of the T-34 has been extensively detailed elsewhere, and this account will focus on the

The T-34 Model 1941 appeared in small numbers on the Finnish Front in 1941; this example was captured between Kaukola and Räisälä on 14 August 1941 and shows the standard configuration built in Stalingrad, with the 34.30. sb-10 narrow welded turret and the 76mm F-34 gun. One T-34 nearby was hit 109 times with only eight penetrations. (SA-kuva)

mid-war years that resulted in the versions that saw combat in Finland in 1944.) By the summer of 1944, there were two principal versions of the T-34 in service: the T-34 Model 1943 was still armed with the 76mm F-34 gun introduced in 1941; the new T-34-85, featuring an enlarged turret and an 85mm gun, made its combat debut in March 1944.

The Sturmgeschütz III (StuG III) assault gun was the principal infantry support vehicle of the Wehrmacht, serving in the same role as the infantry tanks used by other armies in World War II. Although it was originally armed with a short 7.5cm gun for direct fire support, the threat posed by the T-34 in 1941–42 prompted the Wehrmacht to shift to a longer 7.5cm gun that was suitable both for fire support and anti-tank missions.

While it might seem awkward to compare a tank with a turret and an assault gun with a fixed casemate, both the T-34 and StuG III, though they might not have been technically similar, were widely used in the infantry support role; and because both types were manufactured in such large numbers, they frequently saw combat against one another on the battlefields of the Eastern Front. Indeed, StuG III units claimed to have knocked out 20,000 Soviet tanks, the majority of which were T-34s.

The theatre of combat selected for this book is one of the lesser known campaigns of the war: the battles between the Red Army and the Finnish Army in the summer of 1944 during the Continuation War (June 1941–September 1944). Finland was allied with Germany in 1941–44, and had been equipped with the StuG III in 1943. In the summer of 1944, Stalin decided to knock Finland out of the war once and for all. As part of the summer 1944 offensives along the Baltic, the Red Army staged a massive

The Finnish Army generally referred to its assault guns by the early German designation of Stu.40, or by the nickname 'Sturmi'. This is the crew of Sturmi Ps. 531-9 'Toini' with gunner Lance Corporal Kalle Muona in the commander's hatch and loader Pentti Laitinen to the left. This view shows the Finnish use of captured Soviet DT machine guns over the loader's hatch instead of the usual German MG 42. This photo was taken near Enso on 4 June 1944 when the battalion conducted a display for Marshal Carl Mannerheim, commander-in-chief of Finland's defence forces during World War II, and President Risto Ryti. (SA-kuva)

Sturmi Ps. 531-1 'Aune' was the command vehicle of Captain Werner von Troil, leader of the 2nd Company of the Assault Gun Battalion. This was one of the assault guns knocked out by Soviet artillery fire at Kuuterselkä on the morning of 15 June 1944. (SA-kuva)

assault on the Karelian Isthmus, the intention being to eliminate any remaining German and Finnish forces facing the Leningrad region. The focus of this book is the first large-scale armoured clash of the campaign, during which the 185th Separate Tank Regiment – one of several Red Army armoured units involved and a type of unit earmarked for the infantry support role – engaged the Finnish Army's Assault Gun Battalion in a series of skirmishes around Kuuterselkä on 14–15 June 1944.

The T-34-85 saw its combat debut on the Finnish front during the Vyborg offensive. Most if not all T-34-85 tanks taking part in the offensive were of the newer configuration with the improved 85mm ZIS-S-53 gun developed at Nizhni Tagil. This T-34-85 served with the 226th Separate Tank Regiment and was lost on 12 July 1944 during the fighting near Vuosalmi. It was towed away by Finnish troops for repair and then put into Finnish service. (SA-kuva)

CHRONOLOGY

1936

June   The *Sturmgeschütz* development contract is awarded to Daimler-Benz.

1940

January   The first series-production StuG III is completed.

January   The first two A-34 (T-34) prototypes are completed in Kharkov.

May   The StuG III makes its combat debut in France and the Low Countries.

September   Initial serial production of the T-34 with short 76mm L-11 gun is undertaken.

1941

January   The Stalingrad Tractor Factory begins T-34 assembly.

February   Production of the T-34 with the longer 76mm F-34 gun commences.

July   Plans are initiated to evacuate Soviet tank plants to the Urals.

September   The third T-34 factory (No. 112) opens at the Krasnoe Sormovo plant in Gorkiy.

October   Factory No. 183 in Kharkov is closed following evacuation.

December   Factory No. 183 gradually resumes tank production in Nizhni Tagil.

1942

January   Production starts in Nizhni Tagil of the T-34 with the enlarged and simplified Gaika turret.

February   The first StuG III Ausf F with L/43 gun is completed.

June   The frontal armour of the StuG III is increased to 80mm.

June   Development work begins on the T-43 universal tank at Nizhni Tagil.

December   StuG III Ausf G production begins.

1943

February   StuG III production begins at MIAG in Braunschweig.

February   The Sturmhaubitze 42 (StuH 42) enters production at Alkett near Berlin.

15 February   The Finnish Assault Gun Battalion is formed.

June   The Finnish cadre arrives in Germany to train on the StuG III.

30 June   The 185th Separate Tank Regiment is formed by the Red Army.

6 July   The first StuG III is delivered to Finland.

1944

January   Serial production of the T-34-85 with D-5T gun begins at Krasnoe Sormovo.

March   Serial production of the T-34-85 with ZIS-S-53 gun begins at Nizhni Tagil.

9 June   The Red Army's Vyborg operation against Finland begins.

14 June   The battle of Kuuterselkä commences.

24 June   The battle of Tali-Ihantala commences.

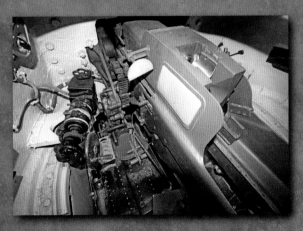

An interior view of a Gaika turret on a T-34 Model 1942 tank.

DESIGN AND DEVELOPMENT

THE T-34

The T-34 made its combat debut in June 1941 when it was committed against the Wehrmacht during Operation *Barbarossa*, the German invasion of the Soviet Union. Combat use of the T-34 in 1941 revealed it to be an exceptionally fine design, with an excellent balance of firepower, mobility and armour protection. Early combat included limited use on the Finnish Front in the summer of 1941 when the Finnish 10th Infantry Division first encountered Red Army T-34s at Räisälä (now Melnikovo) on 14 August 1941 as recorded in their report:

> The men of 2nd Company, 2nd Infantry Regiment were surprised by new 27-ton tanks, none of which were knocked out by our anti-tank guns. They effortlessly passed through our defensive lines, and destroyed several cars and horses with their gunfire. At the clearing at Julya-Vorne, one of the tanks turned around and came back on the same road, further ignoring AT gunfire and Kasapanos mines [satchel charges]. After [14 August], one of these tanks was destroyed, and another broke down, and was captured intact. It was then discovered that these new tanks were T-34s, covered everywhere by thick and reliable sloped armour plates. When the tank was closely examined, 105 dents from anti-tank guns were found. Only two or three shells hit between the wheels and penetrated the armour behind them, as a result of which the tank caught fire and was destroyed.

In spite of its many advantages, the T-34 design had a number of shortcomings. These were addressed by a comprehensive redesign in 1941, called the T-34M, which was strongly influenced by the German PzKpfw III medium tank, an example of which the Soviet Union had purchased during the short-lived alliance with Germany in 1939–40. The T-34M replaced the Christie suspension with torsion-bar suspension, which resulted in a considerable saving in internal hull volume, especially in the fighting compartment. The T-34M also introduced a three-man turret and a commander's vision cupola, reflecting this important German tactical innovation. In the event, the T-34M never proceeded beyond paper studies, due to the crisis in the Soviet tank industry after the launch by the Wehrmacht of Operation *Barbarossa* on 22 June 1941. Because of the speed of the German advance across the Soviet Union, two of the principal Soviet tank factories in Kharkov and Leningrad had to be evacuated to the Urals, along with many of the subsidiary manufacturing plants.

The closure of Factory No. 183 in Kharkov in October 1941 might have halted T-34 production altogether except for the fact that two other plants had begun T-34 production earlier that year. The Stalingrad Tractor Factory (STZ: Stalingradskiy Traktorniy Zavod) began assembling the T-34 in January 1941. This facility did not have the capability to construct the main armoured components such as hulls and turrets, however, and so these components were provided from the neighbouring Shipyard No. 264 (Stalingradskiy sudoverf) and Factory No. 183 in Kharkov prior to the evacuation of the latter plant. The Stalingrad plants helped take up the slack when the Kharkov plant was closed in October 1941. Factory No. 183 was re-established in Nizhni Tagil in December 1941 as the Urals Tank Factory (Uralskiy Tankoviy Zavod), but it took time to ramp up production. Owing to the success of the T-34, other plants were gradually converted to T-34 production, starting with Factory No. 112 at the Krasnoe Sormovo plant in Gorkiy (now Nizhni Novgorod) in September 1941.

The need to re-establish the Soviet tank industry in late 1941 and early 1942 put an enormous strain on Soviet resources; and the factory crisis forced the Red Army to minimize design changes to the T-34 in order to focus on quantity production rather

The 34.30.sb-9 cast turret remained in production at Factory No. 183 in Nizhni Tagil throughout early 1942 while the plant began quantity production of the new Gaika turret. This is a tank from the spring 1942 production batch that was sent to Aberdeen Proving Ground in the United States in the summer of 1942.

9

than quality improvements. Changes that facilitated production were permitted, but extensive improvements, such as the T-34M project, were cancelled. A number of modest changes were made to the T-34 hull including a simplified driver's hatch and a simpler round rear access hatch over the transmission.

One of the few major design changes permitted in late 1941 was the development of a new turret, nicknamed the 'Gaika' (hex nut) because of its shape. The new turret had the factory designation of 34.30.sb.12, which referred to its main assembly drawing: '34' indicated the tank type; '30' indicated the sub-components, in this case the turret; 'sb' was the abbreviation for *sborka* (assembly) and the numerical suffix was the specific modification of the basic assembly. Variants of the basic assembly received a further numerical suffix, e.g. 34.30.sb.12-1.

The early welded T-34 turret was made up of curved, rolled armour plates and was extremely complicated to fabricate. The initial solution to this problem was to manufacture the 34.30.sb.9 cast-armour turret alongside the 34.30.sb.10 welded turret. The cast-armour turret entered production in March–April 1941 at the Mariupol foundry in Ukraine. However, the design was needlessly complicated to cast and in the event, the Mariupol plant had to be evacuated due to the German advance. In August 1941, Factory No. 183 in Kharkov began development of a much simpler hexagonal turret that avoided the complex forward shape of the existing narrow turrets. The new 34.30.sb.12 Gaika turret had increased internal volume to provide the crew with a more acceptable working space. The awkward one-piece turret hatch of the narrow turrets was replaced by two small hatches on the roof. This project was temporarily upset by the evacuation of Factory No. 183 from Kharkov to Nizhni Tagil, but resumed in November 1941.

Instead of producing both welded and cast Gaika turrets, Factory No. 183 decided to concentrate on a cast version. An initial batch was completed in December 1941 and used in the assembly of T-34s starting in January 1942. As a result, the T-34 with the Gaika turret is informally known as the T-34 Model 1942. The original casting process for the Gaika turret was very labour-intensive, and so a substantial reconfiguration of the assembly process was undertaken, resulting in an improved hex turret in March 1942. This improved turret design was successful enough that there were plans to switch all T-34 plants from the early narrow turret to the Gaika turret starting on 1 July 1942. In the event, some plants continued to use the narrow turret due to the limited resources available at the casting foundries. For example, Krasnoe Sormovo Factory No. 112 used the narrow turrets into the summer of 1943.

As an alternative to the cast Gaika turret, the Uralmash factory (UZTM: Uralskiy zavod tyazhelogo mashinostroeniya) in Sverdlovsk (now Yekaterinburg) was instructed to develop a stamped turret using their 10,000-ton press. This type of hex turret was nicknamed the 'Formochka', and a total of 2,062 were completed starting in September 1942.

In the summer of 1942, three additional factories were assigned to T-34 production: No. 174 in Omsk, Tankograd (ChTZ: Chelyabinskiy Traktorniy Zavod) in Chelyabinsk and Uralmash in Sverdlovsk. The Stalingrad plants, which had borne the main burden of T-34 production in late 1941 and early 1942, were forced to close in September 1942 at the outset of the fighting for that city. The Stalingrad Tractor Factory became a major battleground in that epic confrontation. As a result of the three new plants, T-34 production more than quadrupled, from 3,016 in 1941 to 12,535 in 1942.

Some modest improvements began to be introduced to address the most serious technical problems with the T-34. The deficient Pomon oil-bath air cleaner was replaced with the Tsiklon (Cyclone) air filter for T-34s produced from about December 1942 at the main Nizhni Tagil plant and from January 1943 at Chelyabinsk. The new air filter was an improvement, but still far from ideal. During the road march of the 5th Guards Tank Army to Prokhorovka in summer 1943, it was necessary for T-34s to halt every 3–5 hours and remove the dust that had accumulated in the filters. A US report produced after 1945 was critical of the Tsiklon's capabilities:

The first T-34 Model 1942 tanks with 34.30.sb-12 Gaika turrets began appearing on the Finnish Front in early 1942. This particular tank ran over a mine east of the Syväri power plant in eastern Karelia on 18 April 1942. It appears to be one of the tanks from the January–February 1942 initial production batch from Factory No. 183 after it was relocated to Nizhni Tagil. (SA-kuva)

> Wholly inadequate engine intake air cleaners could be expected to allow early engine failure due to dust intake and the resulting abrasive wear. Several hundred miles in very dusty operation would probably be accompanied by severe power loss ... Centrifugal separation of dirt from air was abandoned several decades ago in America as being very ineffective in motor vehicle operation.

The main T-34 factory in Nizhni Tagil began work on a substantially improved T-34 in 1942. Designated the T-34S (*Skorostnoy*: high speed), this was an attempt to address two major shortcomings in the T-34 design. First, the four-speed transmission was antiquated, having been little improved since the original Christie tank and BT-2 light tanks of 1930–33. The transmission was a frequent source of T-34 mechanical breakdowns, so an improved five-speed transmission was developed. Second, the Red Army acknowledged the problem with the T-34's cramped turret layout, which hampered the tank commander's situational awareness. The two-man turret was not tactically effective when compared to German three-man turrets, so an enlarged turret was developed for the T-34S with a three-man layout. Trials of prototype T-34S tanks were completed in early June 1942 and were so favourable that in August 1942, the State Directorate of the tank industry (NKTP: Narodniy kommisariat tankovoy promyshlkennosti) recommended that production shift to this turret configuration. In the event, the switch to these new components threatened to reduce the pace of T-34 production, so introduction of the new transmission was continually delayed and the new three-man turret never entered production. Medium-tank production in the Soviet Union barely kept ahead of combat losses due to the ferocious level of tank attrition at the front in 1942, and Moscow was unwilling to forsake production for the sake of 'disruptive' improvements.

Dynamics of Soviet medium-tank strength				
	1942	**1943**	**1944**	**1945**
Tank strength (1 January)	800	7,600	9,200	12,400
Total losses	6,600	14,700	13,800	7,500
Tank production	12,527	15,840	14,715	10,493
Lend Lease medium-tank deliveries	848	633	2,345	815

Soviet industry succeeded in churning out the T-34 in ever greater numbers, and the use of improved production techniques reduced the man-hours required to manufacture a single T-34 (see accompanying chart). Production costs also fell dramatically, with a T-34 costing R429,256 in 1941, R249,272 in 1942 and R166,310 in 1943.

Man-hours per T-34 tank 1942–45					
Factory	**1 January 1942**	**1 January 1943**	**1 January 1944**	**1 January 1945**	**1 July 1945**
No. 183	5,300	5,100	3,617	3,251	3,209
No. 112	9,000	7,500	5,497	4,439	3,388
No. 174	8,092	7,205	4,574	3,209	3,094

The second major design effort was the T-43 medium tank that entered development in Nizhni Tagil in June 1942. The T-43 was an attempt to create a universal tank combining the heavier armour of KV heavy tanks within the smaller size of a T-34 medium tank. This programme took advantage of the turret and transmission innovations of the T-34S, but introduced much heavier armour – up to 90mm on the turret – as well as other innovations considered for the abandoned T-34M of 1941 such as torsion-bar suspension. Otherwise, the T-43 shared about 70 per cent of its components with the basic T-34 Model 1943. A series of extensive automotive trials were undertaken during the spring of 1943.

At the time of the battle of Kursk, Red Army tank units were still equipped with the same versions of the T-34 that had undergone few major design changes since the summer of 1942. If anything, the focus on production quantity over quality and the increased use of a semi-skilled labour force had led to a deterioration of production quality.

The fighting at Kursk revealed that the T-34 had finally met its match in the new Panther medium tank and Tiger heavy tank. Both of these German designs were considerably larger and heavier than the T-34, and enjoyed advantages in both firepower and armour. Most alarmingly, both tanks were nearly invulnerable to gunfire from the T-34 during frontal engagements, while the more powerful guns on the German tanks could destroy the T-34 from nearly any practical battle range. By August 1943, the Red Army's tank force was clamouring for a 'longer arm' – a new tank gun to restore the balance. The earlier demands for greater armour protection were set aside, and the T-43 universal tank programme was shelved.

The experimental T-34S introduced a three-man turret and an improved five-speed transmission, but serial production was rejected due to the disruption it would have caused to Soviet tank production in 1942.

With T-34 production finally exceeding combat losses, some design improvements were accepted for production. The five-speed transmission developed under the T-34S programme was substituted for the older type towards the end of 1943 at the Chelyabinsk and Sverdlovsk plants. It was slower to be adopted at the main Nizhni Tagil plant, which lacked the necessary machine tools.

The firepower of the T-34 was improved with the adoption of HVAP (high velocity armour piercing) ammunition. This type of ammunition used a very hard and dense tungsten-carbide slug encased in a lightweight aluminium casing. The Red Army called this a sub-calibre projectile (*podkaliberniy*) because the tungsten-carbide core was of a smaller diameter than the gun bore. These rounds were much lighter than conventional steel projectiles and so had a higher muzzle velocity and a greater degree of penetration. Owing to the priority that had been assigned to producing HVAP ammunition for the 45mm anti-tank gun in 1942–43, however, the 76mm BR-354P round was not ready until April–May 1943 and was not in widespread service until October that year.

Although a commander's vision cupola had been developed by June 1942 for the Gaika turret, the cupola was not authorized for production due to the restrictions on non-essential upgrades. In the autumn of 1942, an effort was undertaken to copy the British traversable tank periscope for Soviet tank use due to its versatility and low cost. The Soviet periscope was named the MK-4, after the Vickers Tank Periscope Mark IV periscope sight. Although the commander's cupola, now fitted with the MK-4, was accepted for production at Nizhni Tagil on 7 June 1943, production was delayed until the autumn of 1943, due to an initial lack of MK-4 sights. As with the HVAP ammunition, it was the tank battles at Kursk in July 1943 that persuaded the Soviet authorities to appreciate the urgency of upgrading the T-34's cupola and periscope.

There was a greater effort in 1943 to impose quality control at the tank plants, but complaints continued to escalate about the level of mechanical failures suffered during road marches. To address this issue, it was decided that the Red Army would accept each T-34 only once it had passed a 30km test run at the plant, followed by a 50km

The Gaika turret changed the roof-hatch arrangement from the large single-piece hatch found on the early narrow-turret T-34 tanks to a pair of smaller hatches, as shown here.

test conducted by the military inspectors. To further ensure tank durability, one tank in every 100 was required to carry out a 300km test run (300km was the T-34's warranty endurance at this time). During the first batch of tests, undertaken in April 1943, only 10.1 per cent of the tanks completed the test; and the June 1943 tests saw only 7.7 per cent of the tanks pass the test.

The quality-control problems varied from one plant to another. In May 1943, the five T-34 production plants were each required to provide five new T-34s to participate in endurance trials. While the T-34s from Uralmash reached 1,001km in 4.9 days of operation before breakdowns, the tanks from the Chelyabinsk plant managed only 409km in 2.8 days of operation; the average endurance across the five plants' contributions was 710km. Once the technical upgrades and improvements in quality control had taken place, the durability of new-build T-34s improved. By December 1943, 83.6 per cent of the tanks tested completed the 300km test run.

The drive to improve quality control paid off; having been 8.6 per cent in 1942, combat losses due to mechanical breakdowns decreased to about 2 per cent during the Kursk campaign. For example, the 5th Guards Tank Army was able to move 330–380km on 7–9 July 1943, in a forced march that would have caused excessive T-34 breakdowns in 1942. By early 1944, T-34 reliability finally reached acceptable levels: during February 1944 tests, 79 per cent of tanks reached 300km, and 33 per cent reached 1,000km before a breakdown. The deputy commander of the 1st Guards Tank Army, General Major Pavel G. Dyner, commented that T-34s built in 1943 would reach only 75 per cent of their guaranteed life span in engine hours and distance travelled, but in 1944 they reached 150 per cent.

The lessons of the Kursk campaign prompted efforts to upgrade the T-34's main armament. In mid-1943 the Gaika turret was fitted with the long 57mm ZiS-4 gun. The

Percentage of T-34 tanks reaching 300km during factory trials										
Apr 43	May 43	Jun 43	Jul 43	Aug 43	Sep 43	Oct 43	Nov 43	Dec 43	Jan 44	Feb 44
10.1	23.0	7.7	28.6	43.0	46.0	78.0	57.0	83.6	83.4	79.0

T-34 MODEL 1943, 185th SEPARATE TANK REGIMENT

Crew: 4
Weight: 29.1 tonnes
Length: 5.92m
Width: 3.0m
Height: 2.4m
Engine: 500hp V-2 diesel
Fuel: 465 litres + external (variable)

Maximum speed: 55km/h
Road range: 300km
Main gun: 76mm F-34
Ammunition: 77 rounds

5.92m

2.4m

3.0m

The T-43 was a deep modernization of the T-34 that introduced heavier armour, a three-man turret and many other improvements. Serial production was rejected after the battle of Kursk when the emphasis shifted to the need for a more potent tank gun.

ZiS-4's anti-armour performance was much better than that of the F-34, but the 57mm gun's high-explosive capability was poor compared to the 76mm gun; it was planned to issue the 57mm gun on a scale of about one tank in five. Another possibility was to lengthen the existing 76mm gun, but tests of the L/50 F-34M gun found that it improved anti-armour penetration by only 20–30 per cent. (Barrel length is measured in calibres, so a 76mm L/50 gun is 50×76mm or 3,800mm.) The lengthened S-54 gun, based on an anti-aircraft gun, was examined as another alternative, but the performance improvement it offered was not sufficient to justify fielding another family of 76mm ammunition.

As it happened, the 85mm D-5T gun was ready for production on the new KV-85 heavy tank. A D-5T gun was duly mounted in a Gaika turret, but the small internal volume of the turret was insufficient for such a massive weapon. The eventual solution was to use a universal turret developed for a version of the T-43 tank. This turret housed a three-man crew with a vision cupola for the commander, and was large enough to accommodate an 85mm gun. It had thicker armour than the Gaika turret and added only 1.3 tons to the T-34's weight. The hull roof had to be redesigned, with the turret ring diameter increased from 1.46m to 1.6m to accommodate the new turret. The Soviet tank industry had a very limited capacity to machine wide turret rings, however, until the arrival of additional machine tools via Lend Lease from the United States in early 1944. It was also recognized that the D-5T was only a temporary solution because it was too heavy and bulky for a medium tank, so other gun design efforts were under way.

The first version of the T-34-85 tank armed with the D-5T gun was developed at the Krasnoe Sormovo plant as a stop-gap until an improved and lightened 85mm gun was developed. Between December 1943 and April 1944 a total of 255 of this version of the T-34-85 were built; it made its combat debut in Ukraine during March 1944. Nizhni Tagil developed the definitive version of the T-34-85 in which the improved 85mm ZIS-S-53 gun was mated with Nizhni Tagil's improved 34.30.sb.19-2 turret. This configuration entered production in March 1944. Production of the 85mm

T-34 production by factory

T-34	1941	1942	1943	1944	1945*	Total
Kharkov/Nizhni Tagil No. 183	1,585	5,684	7,485	1,935	0	16,689
Stalingrad STZ	1,256	2,520	0	0	0	3,776
Krasnoe Sormovo No. 112	179	2,584	2,962	557	0	6,282
Uralmash	0	267	452	0	0	719
Omsk No. 174	0	417	1,347	1,163	0	2,927
Tankograd	0	1,055	3,594	445	0	5,094
T-34-85	**1941**	**1942**	**1943**	**1944**	**1945***	**Total**
Nizhni Tagil No. 183	0	0	0	6,553	6,298	12,851
Krasnoe Sormovo No. 112	0	0	0	3,062	2,655	5,717
Omsk No. 174	0	0	0	1,000	1,540	2,540
Total	*3,020*	*12,527*	*15,840*	*14,715*	*10,493*	*56,595*

*First three quarters of year.

BR-365P tungsten-carbide HVAP ammunition commenced in February 1944, with a standard combat load of 5–6 rounds per T-34-85.

The Finnish Army first encountered the T-34-85 in the summer 1944 fighting and captured a few intact tanks. In general, they found the T-34-85 to be a considerable advance over the earlier T-34:

The new Russian T-34 tank armed with an 85 mm gun has the following differences compared to Model 1942 and 1943 tanks. The armor is mostly the same design and same thickness. The hull in general has no advantages over the precursor. The turret is roomier. The armor is improved in the front. It resists 47–75 mm guns well at medium and long range. The sharper shape of the front increases the chance that armor piercing shells will ricochet. The quality of armor is higher than on the model 1943 tank. The diesel engine is the same type, but of better manufacturing quality; it is 20–30 hp more powerful, and has a longer lifespan under medium loads. The oil system is of the same type, but oil consumption is reduced by 30–40%. The exhaust is less smoky. The air filter does its job. In the summer, the diesel engine overheats less, in the winter, it starts more easily. The electrical equipment has isolated copper wiring. The 85 mm gun is a compact tank gun, identical to the German 88 mm tank gun in main parameters, losing out slightly in range and trajectory due to superior quality of German propellant. Compared to the 75 mm tank gun, the new Soviet gun has superior armor piercing and high explosive capability. The design of the gun is very good. It is smaller than the German 75 and 88 mm guns. The design is simple. It surpasses the 76 mm gun in flat shot range by 1.5–2 times. The new radio is very compact and reliable. The quality of communication at short ranges is improved. It is located in the turret and does not require a separate crew member to operate. The new T-34 tank is significantly different from the previous model, not only in armament, but in terms of general combat characteristics. Drawbacks of this tank include the control system, suspension, and transmission. Currently, this type of tank is one of the best medium tanks, on par with new German tanks.

OVERLEAF

The first version of the T-34-85 built at Factory No. 112 in Krasnoe Sormovo used the 85mm D-5T gun. Although it was not as effective as either the Panther's long 7.5cm gun or the Tiger I's 8.8cm gun, the D-5T was able to defeat either German tank under the right operational circumstances. In addition, because the new turret and gun were based on a virtually unchanged T-34 chassis, the T-34-85 did not upset Soviet tank production to the extent that the costly new Tiger and Panther had done to German industry. The D-5T was replaced by the more efficient 85mm ZIS-S-53 gun in the spring of 1944 at Nizhni Tagil and other tank-production plants. This is a column of tanks of the 119th Rifle-Tank Regiment moving to the front on 20 March 1944. The tanks were named after Armenian national hero David Sasunkiy and paid for by contributions from Armenian citizens.

The appearance of the T-34-85 in March 1944 did not cancel out the German advantage in tank technology but did substantially restore the balance. Although the T-34-85 was still not evenly matched against the Panther, the Soviet tank was fielded in far larger numbers than the Panther. By late May 1944, while the Germans had only 304 Panthers in the East, roughly 1,200 T-34-85 tanks were being produced every month, with some 7,200 available at the beginning of the Soviet offensives of summer 1944. While the T-34-85 rarely encountered the Panther, the Soviet tank's gun proved to be very effective against the older German tanks and assault guns such as the PzKpfw IV and StuG III that equipped much of Germany's armoured forces on the Eastern Front.

A computer program developed by the Soviet Army after 1945 modelled and compared the combat performance of various tanks. The table below shows the Soviet Army's assessment of the major Soviet and German tank types in service in 1944, using the PzKpfw III armed with the 5cm L/60 gun as the baseline AFV.

Comparative combat value 1943–45					
PzKpfw III	T-34	PzKpfw IV	T-34-85	IS-2M	Panther
1.0	1.16	1.27	1.32	1.66	2.37

THE StuG III

The StuG III assault gun was developed to provide German infantry with an infantry gun that was more mobile than towed cannon. It eventually evolved into the German infantry's main form of armoured support, essentially the German equivalent of the

Early versions of the StuG III were armed with the short 7.5cm L/24 gun. The StuG III saw its combat debut during the Battle of France in the summer of 1940. However, it was a very rare beast at this point in time, with only four StuG batteries operational.

infantry tanks found in other armies. The StuG III was the inspiration of Erich von Manstein, one of Germany's premier field commanders during World War II. Having served as an infantryman in World War I, Manstein was well aware of the difficulties German infantry confronted when attacking in the face of enemy machine-gun nests and other defence works. The solution to this problem in World War I was the deployment of accompanying small field guns that were light enough that they could be pushed forward by the infantry without the need for horses.

At the outset of World War II, German infantry regiments had a gun company equipped with six of the small 7.5cm leIG 18 light infantry guns and two of the larger horse-drawn 15cm sIG 33 heavy infantry guns. While these guns were better than nothing, they were difficult to move across shell-scarred terrain. Manstein envisioned a self-propelled, armoured accompanying gun that he called *Sturmartillerie*, or assault artillery. This was a reference to the elite German infantry troops of World War I, the Storm Troops, who were used to spearhead the infantry attack. *Sturmartillerie* were not expected to completely replace infantry guns, but rather to support the spearhead of the attacking infantry. After convincing the Army commander-in-chief of the merit of this idea, Daimler-Benz was awarded a development contract in June 1936.

The *Sturmgeschütz* programme was hindered by the limitations of the German armoured-vehicle industry. Tank production up to 1936 had focused on inexpensive, lightly armoured tanks such as the PzKpfw I and PzKpfw II that could be quickly built in sufficient numbers to equip the new Panzer divisions. The Spanish Civil War

This is a StuG III Ausf E of Sturmgeschütz-Abteilung 244 near Ivankovo, north of Kiev in October 1941.

of 1936–39 saw the combat debut of the PzKpfw I with Spanish Nationalist forces and their German advisers. The tanks were pitted against Republican forces equipped with the Soviet T-26 light tank as well as the Soviet 45mm anti-tank gun. The fighting in Spain made it clear that machine-gun-armed light tanks such as the PzKpfw I were nearly useless when confronting gun-armed tanks such as the T-26. They also proved to be extremely vulnerable to the new anti-tank guns because their armour was only proof against machine-gun and rifle fire. Many military observers felt that the anti-tank gun would sweep the battlefield of tanks just as machine guns had swept the battlefield of horse cavalry in World War I.

These developments were not entirely unexpected, however, and German Panzer advocates such as General Heinz Guderian had been pushing for a more capable family of tanks, namely the PzKpfw III and the larger PzKpfw IV support tank, both of which had thicker armour and better guns. Production of these new types was still modest in 1938–39 and as a consequence Guderian was critical of any plans to divert German industry to produce artillery vehicles. He was especially critical of the *Sturmgeschütz* programme, because the new assault gun was based on the PzKpfw III chassis. Guderian criticized Manstein and his supporters on the General Staff, such as Oberst Walter Model, as 'the grave-diggers of the Panzer force' for trying to divert precious industrial resources away from tanks in favour of infantry support weapons.

The new army commander, Generaloberst Walther von Brauchitsch, decided to scale back the *Sturmgeschütz* programme. Instead of an assault-gun battalion in each infantry division, the new force would be limited to a smaller number of units, all assigned at field army level. As a result, no assault-artillery units were ready in time for the September 1939 invasion of Poland. At the time of the invasion of France in May–June 1940, only four *Sturmgeschütz* batteries had been deployed; but their performance in France was exceptional enough that permission was granted to expand the force as and when additional industrial resources became available.

The initial production version of the StuG III was armed with a short 7.5cm L/24 cannon. This was the same armament used on the PzKpfw IV Ausf D tank, and offered performance similar to that of the 7.5cm light infantry gun. Only 95 StuG III were completed up to the beginning of 1941, however. Encounters with the new Soviet T-34 and KV tanks during Operation *Barbarossa* in June 1941 came as a great shock to the German infantry. The common 3.7cm anti-tank gun was ineffective against these heavily armoured tanks, and became derisively known as the 'door knocker'. Even the new 5cm PaK 38 was ineffective in a frontal engagement against the Red Army's armoured monsters. Infantry units were defenceless against this new threat, and 'tank panic' was a frequent result.

The infantry tank panic of the summer of 1941 led to a general reconsideration of infantry support weapons. Rheinmetall/Borsig had already developed a longer L/41 7.5cm gun that was experimentally mounted on a StuG III in the winter of 1940/41. The L/41 gun expanded the mission capabilities of the StuG III, giving it significantly better anti-tank performance while retaining its excellent high-explosive firepower. The L/41 gun was duly lengthened to L/43 to improve its anti-tank performance and was fitted to the new StuG III Ausf F which entered production in February 1942.

In spite of Guderian's continued resistance to devoting Panzer industry resources to this artillery weapon, the need for armoured support for the infantry was a clear

requirement in the eyes of most German commanders. Hitler received glowing reports of the excellent performance of the StuG III in Russia and began to see it as a critical ingredient in creating mobile pockets of resistance to reinforce the embattled infantry. Hitler also encouraged the Army to reinforce the StuG III's armour protection to 80mm to better resist Soviet 76mm guns. This was accomplished by bolting additional 30mm plates to the front starting in late June 1942. By April 1943, the Alkett (Altmärkische Kettenwerk) plant near Berlin was building StuG III with single 80mm front plates. Hitler also supported the enhancement of the StuG III firepower to parallel the improvement process on the Pzkpfw IV tank with a new L/48 7.5cm gun. This was known as the KwK 40 in its tank version and the StuK 40 in its assault-gun version. The new L/48 resulted in the StuG III Ausf G – the definitive version of the StuG III assault gun – that entered production in December 1942.

The success of the StuG III on the Eastern Front prompted a shift of industrial resources and led to an increase in assault-gun battalions. Monthly production at the beginning of 1942 was a mere 45, but by year's end this had nearly tripled to 120 per month. Another reason for the shift in resources was the growing obsolescence of the PzKpfw III on which the StuG III was based. The PzKpfw III was in many ways a superior automotive chassis to the PzKpfw IV due to its more modern torsion-bar suspension. However, its narrower hull limited the size of its turret ring and correspondingly, its main armament. While it could accommodate the longer 5cm gun and the short 7.5cm L/24 gun, it could not be readily adapted to take the 7.5cm L/48 gun in use on the StuG III and PzKpfw IV. Furthermore, the StuG III was more

The short L/24 gun made way for the longer L/43 gun on the StuG III Ausf F for better anti-armour performance. This is a StuG III Ausf F of Sturmgeschütz-Abteilung 210 supporting a German infantry unit in the Kuban region of southern Russia in the summer of 1942.

German AFV production by type 1941–44							
	Panzer	(%)	Sturmgeschütz	(%)	Panzerjäger	(%)	Total
1941	3,256	85.7	540	14.2	0	0	3,796
1942	4,278	69.5	748	12.1	1,123	18.2	6,149
1943	5,966	55.5	3,406	31.6	1,375	12.7	10,747
1944	9,161	50.1	8,682	47.4	441	2.4	18,284

economical of industrial resources than comparable tanks. For example, the StuG III Ausf G cost RM82,500 while the PzKpfw III Ausf M cost RM103,100 and the PzKpfw IV Ausf G cost RM125,000.

As a result of these factors, when the 'Adolf Hitler Armoured Vehicle Programme' was unveiled in September 1942, StuG III production again saw a substantial increase with plans to boost production to 300 per month by March 1944. In order to accommodate this increase, StuG production was extended from its Alkett main plant to the MIAG (Mühlenbau und Industrie Aktiengesellschaft) plant in Braunschweig in February 1943. Assault guns gradually took up a larger and larger share of German AFV production, nearly matching tank production by 1944. Likewise, *Panzerjäger* production was curtailed because the StuG III proved to be an efficient dual-role weapon with excellent anti-tank capabilities.

The StuG III was successful enough that a pilot version of the PzKpfw IV tank with the StuG III superstructure was constructed in 1943. When the Alkett plant was heavily bombed in October 1943, Hitler ordered that production of the StuG IV begin in order to make up the shortages. Krupp ended PzKpfw IV production in December 1943 and switched to StuG IV production in January 1944.

The most significant variant of the StuG III was the Sturmhaubitze 42 (StuH 42) assault howitzer. There had been discussions as early as 1941 to increase the firepower of the StuG III by substituting a 10.5cm lFH 18 in place of the 7.5cm gun; but when the longer L/43 gun replaced the short L/24 gun, the howitzer plan was put into limbo. The programme was revived in late 1942 and the StuH 42 was demonstrated to Hitler, who proved enthusiastic about the programme. The infantry also voiced their approval of the concept, because the gradual shift in focus in the StuG III armament towards weapons with better anti-tank performance tended to distort the use of the assault guns from general infantry fire-support to the anti-tank mission, so there was some interest in refocusing the StuG III back to its original mission. The

StuG III/IV and StuH 42 manufacture 1940–45							
	1940	1941	1942	1943	1944	1945	Total
StuG III L/24	183	541	90				814
StuG III L/43			118				118
StuG III L/48			571	2,934	3,894	863	8,262
StuG IV				30	1,006	105	1,141
StuH 42				175	931	192	1,298
Total	183	541	779	3,139	5,831	1,160	11,633

StuG III Ausf G, FINNISH ASSAULT GUN BATTALION

Crew: 4
Weight: 23.9 tonnes
Length: 6.77m
Width: 2.95m
Height: 2.16m
Engine: 265hp Maybach HL 129 TRM petrol
Fuel: 310 litres

Maximum speed: 40km/h
Road range: 155km
Main gun: 7.5cm StuK 40
Ammunition: 54 rounds

6.77m

2.16m

2.95m

Sturmgeschütz strength/losses 1941–45					
Month	Strength	Losses*	Month	Strength	Losses*
Jun 41	377	4	Jun 43	1,216	93
Sep 41	479	42	Sep 43	1,716	489
Dec 41	598	49	Dec 43	1,877	574
Mar 42	625	88	Mar 44	2,415	756
Jun 42	697	51	Jun 44	2,804	632
Sep 42	873	89	Sep 44	2,655	1,628
Dec 42	1,039	102	Dec 44	3,105	539
Mar 43	1,111	410	Feb 45	3,607	Not recorded
*Cumulative quarterly total.					

StuH 42 was not intended to replace the StuG III, but rather to supplement it. In a standard 31-gun battalion, 22 were StuG III and nine were StuH 42. Aside from a pre-series batch, StuH 42 production began in February 1943. Finland did not receive the StuH 42, but German assault-gun units that served in Finland did employ this type of vehicle, notably Sturmgeschütz-Brigade 303 in the summer of 1944.

The average availability rate in 1943 for the StuG III was 65 per cent – double that of the Tiger or Panther. The StuG III's superior reliability meant that by the end of August 1943, operational German assault guns (524) outnumbered operational German tanks (484) on the Eastern Front, even though there were more German tanks than assault guns on hand in the East. The number of operational assault guns continued to outnumber that of tanks on the Eastern Front until the end of 1944 due to the assault guns' better reliability.

The StuG III's anti-armour capability was enhanced by the crews' superior training as part of the artillery branch, and their vehicles' fire-control sights, which were superior to those of contemporary German tanks. Not only were the StuG III's sights more powerful than those of the tanks, but also the assault-gun commander was provided with a binocular periscopic sight that aided range-finding, leading the Waffenamt (Weapons Agency) in September 1943 to note that 'The kill rates of assault gun batteries are frequently higher than those of Panzer units even though both

German kill claims against Soviet tanks and AFVs January–April 1944											
	Jan 44	%	Feb 44	%	Mar 44	%	Apr 44	%	Total	%
Panzer	1,401	38.1	853	44.7	122	11.8	820	53.1	3,196	39.2
Anti-tank guns	1,050	28.6	341	17.9	327	31.7	251	16.2	1,969	24.1
Sturmgeschütze and *Panzerjäger*	757	20.6	472	24.7	297	28.8	236	15.3	1,762	21.6
Artillery, mines, other	348	9.4	148	7.7	142	13.7	63	4.0	701	8.6
Other anti-tank weapons	114	3.1	91	4.7	143	13.8	172	11.1	520	6.4
Total	3,670		1,905		1,031		1,542		8,148	

are equipped with the same [7.5cm L/48] main gun.' An August 1943 report to Hitler in the wake of the Kursk battles also praised the StuG III's performance: 'the reports from the front submitted to the Führer highlight the exceptional value of the assault gun which in several cases under the prevailing combat conditions proved superior to the Panzer IV.'

During 1943, as combat operations became more challenging for the Germans, the StuG III significantly bolstered the German infantry's fighting power, essentially becoming the Wehrmacht's infantry tank, even if not officially designated as such. Tank fighting came to be an increasingly important part of the StuG III's combat role by 1943, even though this had not been its original function. *Sturmgeschütz* units claimed 18,261 kills against Soviet AFVs between June 1941 and August 1944 – nearly one-fifth (18 per cent) of all such claims. Even if tank fighting took on added importance in the final years of the war, the primary mission of the StuG III continued to be infantry fire support, with approximately 85 per cent of StuG III ammunition consumption being high-explosive projectiles in this role.

In terms of the costs of production, the StuG III offered the Wehrmacht considerable value for money. The Wehrmacht could have bought ten StuG III for the price of three Tiger tanks. Once the StuG III's superior reliability is factored in, the Wehrmacht could have fielded seven operational StuG III for each operational Tiger.

The later production series of the StuG III Ausf G incorporated a number of changes including the *Saukopf* (pig's head) cast armour mantlet. Finland bought another batch of 29 StuG III from Germany after the start of the Soviet offensive, including this example (Ps. 531-34) from the Alkett (Altmärkische Kettenwerk) plant's May 1944 production batch. Aside from the later mantlet and Alkett-pattern *Zimmerit* anti-mine paste coating, this vehicle has other Finnish changes including concrete armour over the upper superstructure front, lower hull appliqué armour, and log protection on the superstructure side. (SA-kuva)

One of the derivatives of the *Sturmgeschütz* was the *Sturmhaubitze*, intended to provide heavier firepower. This is a StuH 42 of Sturmgeschütz-Brigade 303 that fought in Finland in the summer of 1944. On 14 February 1944 the Wehrmacht designation of the *Sturmgeschütz* battalion (*Abteilung*) was changed to brigade. This confusing development was in fact purely a propaganda move, and there was no change in unit strength. Likewise, the assault-gun companies in the infantry divisions' *Panzerjäger-Abteilungen* were redesignated as battalions. To muddy the waters further, the divisional assault-gun battalions reverted back to the company designation in early October 1944. (SA-kuva)

There were numerous small detail changes to the StuG III Ausf G during the course of its production. One of the most visible was as a result of the decision to fit 5mm-thick armoured *Schürzen* (side skirts) to the vehicles starting in April 1943. *Schürzen* – dubbed 'bazooka skirts' by some Allied troops – had in fact been developed to counter the threat posed by Soviet anti-tank rifles such as the 14.5mm PTRS and PTRD. Although these rifles could not penetrate the StuG III frontally, they could penetrate the vehicle's thinner side armour; but after hitting the *Schürzen*, the rifle projectile tended to yaw or tumble, preventing it from penetrating the main armour. *Schürzen* were regularly fitted to the StuG III Ausf G from April 1943, and saw their first extensive combat use during the Kursk campaign in the summer of 1943. The first batch of Finnish StuG III Ausf G arrived fitted with *Schürzen*, but they were removed by the Finns who felt that they were impractical under local conditions.

One of the recurring tactical issues was the absence of a co-axial machine gun for defence against infantry while the StuG III crew was under cover. A decision was made to add a co-axial machine gun, but this feature did not appear until very late in the production run. MIAG began adding the appropriate mounting in the flat plate mantlet starting in May 1944, and Alkett followed suit in August 1944. Alkett had introduced a cast armour mantlet, often called the *Saukopf* (pig's head), starting in October 1943, and this type of mantlet was modified to take a co-axial machine gun starting in September 1944.

There were several other alternatives for a self-defence weapon including the *Rundumsfeuer* external weapon station and the *Nahverteidigungswaffe* close-defence weapon, but these were of little consequence for the Finnish StuG III because they appeared so late in 1944.

TECHNICAL SPECIFICATIONS

FIREPOWER

The StuG III had superior firepower to the T-34, and comparable firepower to the T-34-85. The F-34 gun of the T-34 was not very effective in penetrating the StuG III frontally using ordinary APCBC (armour piercing capped, ballistic cap) ammunition,

Comparative technical details			
	T-34 Model 1942	T-34-85 Model 1944	StuG III Ausf G
Crew	4	5	4
Dimensions (L×W×H)	5.92m×3.0m×2.4m	8.1m×3.0m×2.7m	6.77m×2.95m×2.16m
Loaded weight	29.1 tonnes	32.2 tonnes	23.9 tonnes
Main gun	76.2mm F-34	85mm ZIS-S-53	7.5cm StuK 40
Main gun ammunition	77	60	54
Engine	500hp	500hp	300hp
Maximum speed	55km/h	55km/h	40km/h
Fuel	465+1,343 litres	815 litres	310 litres
Range (km)	300km	300km	155km
Ground pressure	0.72kg/cm^2	0.83kg/cm^2	0.93kg/cm^2

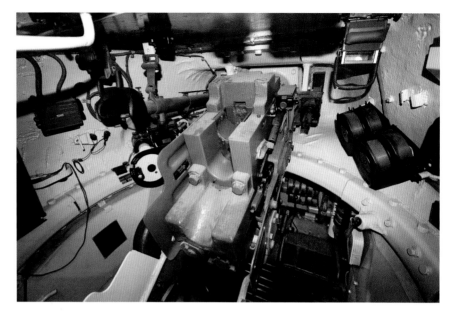

An interior view of a T-34-85 turret viewed from the loader's side looking towards the left and the gunner's station. The gunner's telescopic sight is evident to the left side of the 85mm ZIS-S-53 gun. On the loader's side is a stowage rack for four DT machine-gun ammunition drums, while a MK-4 periscope can be seen emanating from the roof.

but it could penetrate it using HVAP ammunition. The Red Army had a more generous supply of HVAP ammunition than the German and Finnish forces due to extensive tungsten deposits in the Soviet Union. Germany lacked extensive tungsten deposits and thus production of HVAP ammunition fell precipitously in 1943–44 when Britain applied political pressure against neutral countries that were supplying tungsten to Germany, such as Portugal. The 85mm gun on the T-34-85 was similar in performance to the German 7.5cm gun, and could penetrate the StuG III frontally with ordinary ammunition at ranges of about 700m (depending on impact angle), and at longer ranges using HVAP ammunition.

Regarding the balance between high-explosive ammunition and anti-tank ammunition, the 23 StuG III assault-gun brigades on the Eastern Front from 1 December 1943 to 31 May 1944 fired a total of 315,280 rounds of which 263,685 (83.7 per cent) were fired against targets such as infantry, strongpoints and vehicles, while 51,595 (16.3 per cent) were fired against tanks and other armoured targets. It is interesting to note that the 51,595 armour-piercing rounds fired against Soviet tanks and other armoured targets resulted in claims for 1,899 AFVs destroyed as well as 132 disabled. On average, more than 25 rounds of ammunition were fired for each enemy AFV destroyed or disabled.

The T-34-85 standard ammunition load in the Red Army was 55 rounds consisting of a standard load-out of 36 rounds of HE-fragmentation, five rounds of HVAP and 14 rounds of AP (armour piercing). The Finnish StuG III were supposed to be delivered with 1,200 rounds of ammunition consisting of 600 rounds of high explosive (HE), 580 rounds of APCBC and 20 rounds of HVAP. In actuality, the deliveries amounted to only 600 rounds, only ten of which were PzGr 40 tungsten-carbide HVAP.

The StuG III offered excellent anti-tank accuracy due to sighting equipment that was better than that in Soviet tanks. The vehicle commander operated a Scherenfahrlafetten SF.14Z 'scissors' binocular telescope offering 10× magnification; the Soviet tanks lacked such a sight. The Selbstfahrlafetten Zielfernrohr Sfl.ZF1a

T-34 AND StuG III AMMUNITION

1   2   3   4   5   6

Comparative gun performance			
Gun type	76mm F-34	85mm ZIS-S-53	7.5cm KwK 40
Tube length	L/41.6	L/52	L/48
Armour-piercing projectile	BR-350A (**1**)	BR-365	PzGr 39 (**4**)
Type	APCBC	AP	APCBC
Initial muzzle velocity	662m/sec	792m/sec	790m/sec
Projectile weight (kg)	6.3kg	9.02kg	4.1kg
Penetration @500m, 30°	59mm	90mm	91–96mm
Armour-piercing projectile (high velocity)	BR-350P (**2**)	BR-365P	PzGr 40 (**5**)
Type	HVAP	HVAP	HVAP
Initial muzzle velocity	965m/sec	1,030m/sec	930m/sec
Projectile weight	3.02kg	4.99kg	4.1kg
Penetration @500m, 30°	77mm	105mm	108–120mm
High-explosive projectile	OF-350 (**3**)	O-365	SprGr 34 (**6**)
Projectile weight	6.2kg	9.57kg	5.74kg
Explosive fill	490g	775g	653g

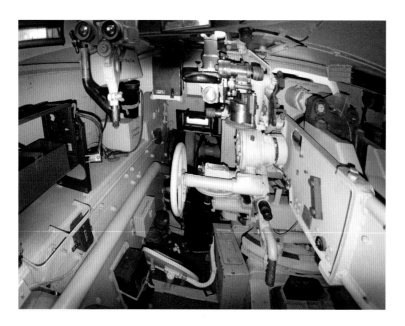

This is an interior view of a restored StuG III Ausf G from Jacques Littlefield's Military Vehicle Technology Foundation in California. This example was originally the Finnish Army's Ps. 531-16. This view was taken from the commander's station looking forward over the gunner's station. The optics from the Scherenfernrohr SF.14Z 'scissors' binocular telescope can be seen in the upper left, while the gunner's Selbstfahrlafetten Zielfernrohr 1a (Sfl.ZF1a) periscopic sight is evident immediately forward in the upper centre. In the lower centre is the gunner's folded seat and the elevation wheel for the 7.5cm gun.

gunner's periscopic sight on the StuG III provided 5× magnification with an 8-degree field of view.

The T-34 gunner had two sights: the TMFD-7 telescopic sight and a PT-4-7 periscopic dial sight; other periscopic dial sights such as the PT-5 and PT-7 were used during the war depending on availability. The TMFD-7 telescopic sight offered 2.5× magnification and a 14.5-degree field of view. Aside from having lower magnification than the German sight, the optical quality of the lenses was mediocre compared to the German devices and permitted only about 39.2 per cent light transmission. The German optics industry was the world leader in lens coatings early in the war which offered superior light transmission through the multiple lenses in the telescope. The Soviet periscopic dial sights mounted on the turret roof were intended to offer a wider field of view for better target acquisition with a 25-degree field of view, but the optical quality of the lenses was even poorer than that of the telescopic sight with a 26.3 per cent light transmission.

The quality issues affecting the Soviet tank sights were addressed in 1943 with the newer tank telescopes such as the TSh-16 used on the T-34-85. The new sights were based on captured German tank telescopic sights. The TSh-16 had a 4× magnification and a 16-degree field of view. A Finnish assessment of this sight noted that: 'the refractive telescope (of the T-34-85) is greatly superior to the sight of the T-34 Model 1942 and 1943 tanks. The clarity of the sight is on the level of the German 75mm PaK 40 anti-tank gun. The reticle is more convenient when firing at tanks up to 1,000m. Injury during motion is nearly impossible due to the comfortable eye-pads.'

Aside from the actual sighting equipment, firing procedures also influenced gun performance. There was considerable controversy in the Wehrmacht over the relative advantages of artillery-style fire controls as well as artillery-crew training for the StuG III. The StuG III crews traditionally used the artillery style of 'bracketing', i.e. firing a first round high, and then adjusting lower until the target was struck. Panzer crews were taught to 'walk' their fire to the target. In comparative tests, the artillery style of 'bracketing' was found to be quicker and more economical.

The most significant difference in firepower between the StuG III and T-34 was in weapons traverse, with the T-34 having an advantage in close combat due to its turret. The StuG III's gun was limited to a traverse of 10 degrees either side of the centreline. This was not a critical disadvantage if the StuG III was in an overwatch or ambush position at long range from its intended target, but it became a significant tactical risk at closer ranges or in fine-grain terrain. On the other hand, the StuG III's low silhouette made the vehicle less visible, and hence less vulnerable, to enemy fire.

Another advantage enjoyed by the T-34 was its more extensive machine-gun armament in the form of a hull-mounted 7.62mm DT machine gun, and a co-axial DT. Both weapons were especially useful when fighting against enemy infantry. The StuG III lacked a co-axial machine gun during most of its production run. The loader was provided with a protective shield intended to be used in conjunction with a 7.92mm MG 42 machine gun for self-defence. (The Finnish Army instead fitted this shield with captured DT machine guns.) However, this position exposed the gunner to fire from the sides, rear and overhead compared to the fully enclosed machine guns on the T-34.

COMMAND AND CONTROL

The retention of two-man turrets such as the Gaika on the earlier versions of the T-34 significantly hampered the successful application of Soviet tank tactics, as this configuration required Soviet tank commanders to juggle their command responsibilities with their gunnery tasks. Moreover, the mediocre optics in Soviet tanks and the standard tactical practice of fighting 'buttoned-up' undermined the tank commanders' situational awareness in combat. The addition of a commander's cupola to the T-34 Gaika turret in the autumn of 1943 improved the commander's vision, but it did not relieve his excessive tasks. The T-34-85's new turret solved both problems by the switch to a three-man turret layout as well as a commander's cupola.

By 1943, most T-34 tanks had a radio transceiver. The 9R radio was introduced in 1942 and was the common type until 1943 when the improved 9RM was introduced.

An interior view of a spring 1942-production T-34 sent to the United States showing the bow-gunner/radio operator station in the right forward hull. The DT machine gun is missing from its mount, but this photo clearly shows the numerous sub-components of the 9R radio transceiver. The pressurized-air cylinder behind the levers is for the air-starting system which was a back-up method for use if the batteries were dead or the starter was broken.

The Sturmi commander sat in the left rear corner of the fighting compartment. This is Staff Sergeant Börje Brotell, who commanded Ps. 531-10 'Bubi', the highest-scoring Sturmi of the campaign. Brotell was one of a number of Finns who served on the Eastern Front with the Finnish Waffen-SS in 1942–43. (SA-kuva)

The 9RM was a modular AM transmitter-receiver (transceiver) type with a power output of 5 watts and used pre-selected channels. When the T-34 was on the move, the 9RM had an effective voice range of about 8km. Communication inside the T-34 was by means of a TPU-3 interphone system. The crew's cloth helmets contained earphones and a small throat microphone. The improved 9RS was introduced in 1944 and used on the T-34-85. Another useful change arising from the T-34-85's layout was the transfer of the radio from the bow-gunner's station to the commander's station. Besides giving the commander greater control over the radio, this transfer eliminated what had been a lingering problem with the radio's previous location, because the bow-gunner/radio operator station was the one most often left vacant as a result of the frequent shortages of crewmen in Red Army tank units. The 9RS was a more compact set, and its position near the tank commander avoided the problem of missing radio operators.

The standard radio fit in the initial batch of Finnish StuG III was the Fu 5, which was a 10-watt short-wave transceiver that operated in the 27.2–33.3MHz bands. The StuG III of platoon and higher commanders had the expanded Fu 8 set which added an additional receiver to monitor a broader range of communication networks. Later batches of StuG III had the FuG 16/FuG 15 option.

PROTECTION

Overall, the StuG III and T-34 had similar levels of armour, with the frontal areas protected by the equivalent of about 90mm of armour plate. The accompanying chart shows the basic armour layout in actual thickness, angle of the plate, and effective

thickness. Effective thickness is an assessment of the armour performance measured by the actual thickness and the effect of the angle of the armour plate. The T-34 had better side armour than the StuG III.

The StuG III Ausf G underwent continual armour upgrades during its manufacture to address the increasing lethality of Soviet anti-tank weapons. Alkett began adding an additional 30mm plate to the existing 50mm armour on the front superstructure and bow in the summer of 1942 and the initial production version of the StuG III Ausf G had this affixed with bolts or by welding. In April–July 1943, the bolted appliqué armour on the bow was replaced by integral 80mm armour plate (the appliqué armour on the superstructure front used this method by the summer of 1944). In October 1943, Alkett introduced a cast steel mantlet for the gun instead of the plate-armour type previously in use; some of the older type of mantlet continued to appear in the production run due to shortages of the new type. Another type of protection upgrade seen in the final years

Comparative armour protection*			
	T-34 Model 1942	T-34-85	StuG III Ausf G
Mantlet	45mm** = >45mm	90mm** = >90mm	80mm @ 0° = 80mm
Turret front	52mm @ 30° = 60mm	90mm** = >90mm	n/a
Turret side	52mm @ 20° = 55.3mm	45mm @ 5° = 45.2mm	n/a
Upper hull front	45mm @ 60° = 90mm	45mm @ 60° = 90mm	80mm @ 10° = 81.2mm
Lower hull front	45mm @ 53° = 73.1mm	45mm @ 60° = 90mm	80mm @ 21° = 85.1mm
Upper hull side	45mm @ 40° = 58.7mm	45mm @ 53° = 73.1mm	30mm @ 0° = 30mm
*Armour data provided as actual thickness in millimetres @ angle from vertical = effective thickness in millimetres.	**Curved		

of the war was the addition of concrete over the front corners of the StuG III. In addition to the integral armour, the StuG III was fitted with *Schürzen* side skirts in the summer of 1943 to defend against Soviet anti-tank rifle fire.

The Finnish StuG III involved in the initial encounters in June 1944 were mainly configured with the 30+50mm frontal armour. The Finns removed the *Schürzen* side skirts originally fitted to the vehicles when delivered, feeling that this feature was impractical. This issue was reconsidered after the early summer fighting once it was recognized that the StuG III hull side was vulnerable to Soviet anti-tank rifle fire. Finnish Army depots added appliqué armour plates to the lower hull, and the upper hull sides were protected by logs.

The T-34 with the Gaika turret had thinner frontal armour than might be expected, but the rounded surface of the trunnion bulges improved the protective quality due to the angle of the surface. The T-34-85 introduced much thicker turret frontal armour in response to advances in German tank gun power, which offered superior protection to that of both the StuG III and T-34 from frontal attack.

The T-34 provides a clear example of the trade-off between the benefits and drawbacks of steeply angled hull armour. Although the T-34's sloped sides reduced the likelihood of the tank being penetrated by enemy projectiles, it also led to a decrease in internal hull volume. In the event the T-34 was penetrated, it was far more likely to lead to catastrophic damage due to the compression of fuel and ammunition in a relatively small space. The side sponsons of the T-34 fighting compartment contained fuel cells which, if penetrated, could lead to fire and the catastrophic destruction of the tank. This was a particular problem if the fuel tanks were partially full.

Armour data provides only part of the picture of a tank's protection, however. Other factors in assessing the vulnerability of a tank include the internal arrangement of fuel and ammunition. Both the StuG III and T-34 stowed most of their ammunition low in the hull, which reduced the probability of it being hit when the vehicle was penetrated. The T-34-85 ammunition layout decreased the survivability of the tank, however, because the larger size of the 85mm shells forced the designers to place a significant portion of the ammunition load – 16 of the 55 rounds – in the turret, where they had a high probability of being hit; the remaining 39 rounds were stowed on the floor or against the lower hull walls, near the loader.

THE COMBATANTS

T-34 CREW

The crew of the T-34 Model 1943 comprised four men. In the hull sat the driver/ mechanic on the left side and a bow machine gunner/radio operator on the right side. The turret crew was two: the tank commander/gunner on the left side and the loader on the right. It was the usual practice for the tank commander to serve as the

The crew stations in the T-34
Model 1943.

The initial T-34 narrow turret was quite cramped, as can be seen in this example with a 34.30.sb-10 welded turret, captured by the Finnish Army in 1941. The commander was stationed on the left side and served as gunner while the loader was on the right. Some T-34s had periscopic sights (shown here) for both the commander and loader, but the loader's periscopic sight was often deleted due to a shortage of the sight's expensive optics. (SA-kuva)

gunner. Soviet tank officers complained that the T-34's commander had to be a 'circus performer', simultaneously directing the crew, aiming the main gun and instructing the driver. German tankers often noted that Soviet tank units were not well coordinated and were slow to locate and engage targets; a tactical shortcoming that was in large measure due to the T-34's archaic turret layout. This shortcoming was finally addressed on the T-34-85, which increased the turret crew to three: the gunner in the forward left side and the tank commander behind him; the loader alone on the right side. The interior of the T-34 and T-34-85 was very austere; crew ergonomics had never been a strong point of Soviet tank design. The T-34 and T-34-85 lacked a turret basket, and the crew sat on seats suspended from the turret ring.

An interesting view of the interior of a T-34 narrow turret under repair at the Finnish Varkaus depot. The interior is dominated by the 76mm F-34 gun, leaving a modest amount of space on either side for the crew. The commander's station, visible at the bottom, has the traversing mechanism for the turret. The rear turret bustle is filled with racks for the co-axial 7.62mm DT machine gun's ammunition drums. This is the variant of the 34.30.sb-10 welded turret (note its distinctive flat rear plate) produced at Shipyard No. 264 in Stalingrad for the nearby Stalingrad Tractor Factory's T-34s. (SA-kuva)

T-34 TURRET

1. Armoured cover for periscopic sight
2. Cupola view slit
3. MK-4 periscopic sight
4. Commander's cupola
5. 76mm F-34 gun breech
6. 76mm ammunition stowage
7. Pistol port
8. Machine-gun ammunition drum stowage
9. Gun protective cage
10. Gunner/commander seat
11. Gun control foot pedals
12. Turret traverse
13. Gun elevation control
14. Gun telescopic sight
15. Gun periscopic sight

The T-34 tank commander usually used the periscopic dial sight for observing terrain. Those tanks fitted with the commander's cupola offered far better visibility because the commander could view the terrain either using the view slits around the base of the cupola, or the MK-4 periscopic sight. It was not Soviet practice for the commander to fight from an open hatch as was the German practice. Indeed, the hatch location, opening to the front, made it extremely difficult if not impossible to do so. Once a target was located, the commander had to switch to the periscopic dial sight or telescopic sight to engage the target; a requirement that slowed the engagement cycle.

In the T-34-85, the commander was freed from the gunnery chores and so could concentrate on directing his tank and locating targets. As in the later models of the T-34, the T-34-85 had a commander's cupola with vision slits at the base and a MK-4 periscope sight on the top. The T-34-85 gunner sat immediately in front of the commander and operated the main 85mm gun and co-axial 7.62mm DTM machine gun based on instructions from the commander. When not in action, the gunner could observe the terrain using the MK-4 above and to the left of the telescopic sight; there was also a small view port at his left shoulder which could be used in conjunction with a pistol port for tank self-defence. The gunner's position provided very poor

A view of the front hull interior of a T-34 Model 1941 with the original style of driver's hatch and periscopes. The positions are for the driver (left) and the bow-gunner (right), and visible is the complex network of rods running along the floor from the driver's controls to the rear-mounted transmission. The DT machine gun is missing from the mount in the upper right. (SA-kuva)

visibility of the surrounding environment and so he depended on instructions from the commander to help him locate the target. Once the target had been identified, the gunner swung the turret into the intended direction with the electro-mechanical turret traverse using his left hand. The electrical turret traverse was not precise enough for fine gun-laying, but it would move the turret quickly into the rough azimuth, at which point the gunner would make final corrections using the mechanical turret traverse. The gunner elevated and depressed the main gun using the mechanical elevation wheel with his right hand. He aimed the tank's 85mm main gun via the TSh-16 telescopic sight and used the stadia in the sight to estimate the range in order to introduce any necessary elevation corrections for either the main gun or the co-axial machine gun. The gunner fired by using a foot-pedal control system in which the left foot pedal triggered the main gun and the right foot pedal triggered the co-axial machine gun. There were also back-up manual triggers for both weapons.

The T-34 loader had a simple seat suspended from leather straps between the turret ring and the gun trunnion. In combat, this seat would be folded up out of the way and the loader would stand on the floor. Both the T-34 and T-34-85 had ready rounds positioned around the hull. The T-34-85 also had a ready rack in the rear of the turret. Once these rounds were expended, the loader would have to extract additional rounds from within the metal boxes stored on the floor which made up the rest of the tank's ammunition reserve. The gunner's job was made all the more difficult by the lack of an easy or safe means to dispose of spent shell casings.

The driver had one of the most demanding and exhausting tasks of any of the T-34 crew due to the relatively simple tractor-style driving controls and the need to activate the rear brakes via mechanical linkages running along the floor to the rear-mounted transmission. To make matters worse, the driver's station was quite small and cramped, so drivers had to be both short in stature and exceptionally strong to endure the rigours of this job. This sometimes led to bad driving practices, such as advancing the gearbox into second gear and adjusting speed by means of the fuel pedal only, not shifting to the upper gears due to the difficulty of doing so. Such practices tended to lead to premature powertrain failures. The driver was also responsible for the maintenance and care of the engine.

Adjacent to the driver on the right side of the hull was the bow-gunner who operated the 7.62mm DT machine gun. This position was also relatively cramped and extremely claustrophobic because the only view of the outside was via a 2× telescopic sight used to aim the machine gun. The lack of a vision cupola in this station made it unlikely that the bow-gunner could identify a target unless it was very obvious. The dubious utility of the DT machine gun meant that this position was the first to be left vacant in the event that the crew was understaffed.

StuG III CREW

The StuG III Ausf G had a crew of four: the gun commander, gunner, loader/radio operator and driver. Three of the crew were located on the left side of the vehicle, while the loader stood on the right side of the gun; all were all connected through a vehicle intercom system via radio headsets and throat mikes. The gun commander was usually a non-commissioned officer and directed the rest of the crew from the left rear corner of the fighting compartment. On the StuG III Ausf G, the commander had a cupola fitted with eight periscopes for all-around vision. His main vision instrument was a 'scissors' binocular telescope which was deployed through a small flap in the crew hatch for better armoured protection. The

The crew stations in the StuG III Ausf G.

The loader in the Sturmi was on the right side of the fighting compartment. This is Armas Launikko, the loader on Ps. 531-10 'Bubi'. (SA-kuva)

A view of the restored Ps. 531-16 showing the loader's station on the right side of the fighting compartment. As can be seen, out of the total of 54 rounds 38 were located in racks in front of the loader. The two frames above the sponson are for the vehicle's second radio set. The second radio set could be a transceiver set or just a receiver depending on the vehicle configuration.

commander was responsible for surveying the terrain for targets, and then instructing the driver to roughly aim the vehicle towards the objective, the gunner of the precise target and range, and the loader the type of ammunition required. The gunner sat immediately in front of the commander and sighted through a periscopic telescope. The gun elevation and traverse controls were manual. In front of the gunner in the front left side of the fighting compartment was the driver, whose vision was restricted to a single armoured glass episcope. The loader stood on the right side of the gun where most of the vehicle ammunition was located. The gunner was also cross-trained in radio operation; the radio was located in the sponson over the right track. In addition, the loader manned the vehicle's machine gun which was located over his station.

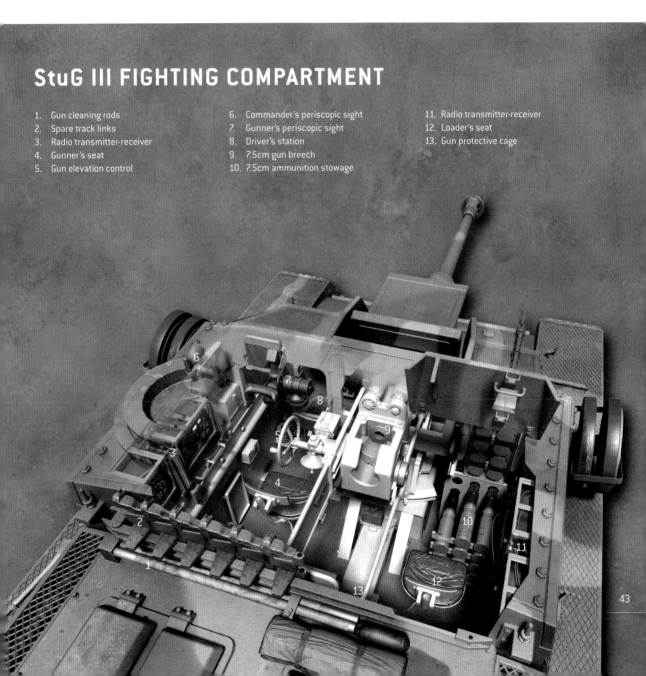

StuG III FIGHTING COMPARTMENT

1. Gun cleaning rods
2. Spare track links
3. Radio transmitter-receiver
4. Gunner's seat
5. Gun elevation control

6. Commander's periscopic sight
7. Gunner's periscopic sight
8. Driver's station
9. 7.5cm gun breech
10. 7.5cm ammunition stowage

11. Radio transmitter-receiver
12. Loader's seat
13. Gun protective cage

A view of the driver's station in the restored StuG III Ausf G Ps. 531-16. In this view, the back of the seat is folded flat to allow the driver to reach the position from the rear.

SOVIET T-34 UNITS IN FINLAND 1944

At the start of June 1944, the Leningrad Front deployed three tank brigades, two Guards heavy-tank breakthrough regiments, four separate tank regiments and a number of assault-gun units. Not all of these units were committed to the initial attack and about half were kept in reserve. The new equipment allotted to the Leningrad Front in May 1944 for the Vyborg (Finnish: Viipuri) operation included 70 new T-34-85 tanks, 42 IS-2 heavy tanks and 63 ISU-152 heavy assault guns. The tank brigades generally contained about 30 T-34s, 20 T-60/T-70 light tanks and four SU-76M self-propelled assault guns, while the separate tank regiments generally included 21 T-34 or T-34-85 tanks. Three of the tank regiments – the 21st, 98th and 226th Separate Tank regiments – were equipped with the T-34-85. (It is possible that

VASILY TENERENTEVICH VASILIEV

Unlike Mauri Sartio, little is known of the career of Vasily Vasiliev beyond the very basic details. He is anonymous, like so many other soldiers of the Red Army in the Great Patriotic War. He was born in 1918 and was recruited into the Red Army in 1939 from the Tula area. He originally served in the 226th Separate Tank Regiment. At the time of the June 1944 Vyborg offensive, he was a Senior Lieutenant and platoon commander in Lieutenant Colonel Aleksandr K. Yunatskiy's 185th Separate Tank Regiment. During the initial breakthrough battle north of Sestroretsk on 10 June, his tank, No. 958, was credited with wiping out a Finnish infantry company, six bunkers, eight machine guns and three mortars. Vasiliev led the attack into Terijoki (now Zelenogorsk). According to a later award citation, Vasiliev and his crew were credited with knocking out a total of seven bunkers and 11 machine guns during the fighting on 10–14 June. During the attack on Kuuterselkä, Vasiliev and his crew managed to find a weak point in the VT Line and pushed through the Finnish defences. This was witnessed by the Red Army front-line correspondent Pavel Luknitsky: 'Suddenly everyone saw this lonely tank bursting into the thick of the defenses. Maneuvering, darting, diving, it crawled between strongpoints. This was tank No. 958, of Senior Lieutenant Vasiliev. By overcoming several defense points, he found himself a narrow passage. Using his radio, he reported: I've found a passage, rally the riflemen and follow me.' Vasiliev's tank was knocked out and he was killed later in the day. It is believed that his tank was one of those knocked out by Mauri Sartio's Sturmi during the initial encounter north of Kuuterselkä. Vasiliev was awarded the For the Defence of Leningrad decoration posthumously on 11 August 1944. After the war, based on the testimony of soldiers who had witnessed his actions at Kuuterselkä, he was awarded the Order of Patriotic War 1st Class (Orden Otechestvennaya Voyna 1 Stepeni). Vasiliev was buried along with many other soldiers from his unit on the hill near Kuuterselkä, where he was killed, and a memorial plaque was erected near the ruins of the VT Line to commemorate his actions that day. Kuuterselkä is now part of the Russian Federation and is known by its Russian name Lebyazhye.

Senior Lieutenant Vasily T. Vasiliev.

several of the other tank units had small numbers of T-34-85 tanks.) Besides the units equipped with the T-34-85, the other tank brigades and tank regiments were generally equipped with new T-34 Model 1942 and Model 1943 tanks fitted with the Gaika turret.

The unit at the centre of this study was the 185th Separate Tank Regiment (185-y otdelniy tankoviy polk). This unit was formed on 30 June 1943 on the basis of the previous 185th Tank Brigade. The 185th Tank Brigade had been formed on 15 February 1942 and served on the Volkhov Front near Leningrad until June 1943 when it was reorganized as a regiment. In its 1943 brigade configuration, it was equipped with a mixture of light and medium tanks; for example, it had 19 T-34, 14 T-60 and six T-70 in January 1943. Under the new regimental structure, it was equipped solely with T-34 tanks and had 21 of the type on strength at the start of the Vyborg offensive. The regiment was commanded by Lieutenant Colonel Aleksandr K. Yunatskiy, who had started the war as a tank battalion commander in the 10th Tank Division.

Very little detail is available regarding the training of the troops of the 185th Separate Tank Regiment, so a general overview of Soviet tank-crew training must suffice. The Red Army had little opportunity to indulge in prolonged tank-crew training due to the high levels of crew casualties and the voracious personnel demands of the many tank formations. The pre-war practice of training tank crews within the unit in special training companies was largely abandoned after the start of the war in favour of new tank training regiments, many of which were set up near the tank factories. To speed up the training process, in the spring of 1942 the Red Army sent out a notice that all troops who had been tractor drivers or who had driving licences must be transferred to the new tank training units. On paper, the training programme was four months long and included basic training followed by technical training. At the end of the programme, the new tank crews were organized into platoons and companies and dispatched to a crash 15-day unit training exercise. This consisted of five days of crew drills, a three-day platoon familiarization course, and finally a four-day company exercise to learn offensive and defensive tactics. Resources were quite limited, so during the platoon exercise, the norm was only 2.5 hours of actual tank driving, three live rounds of tank-gun ammunition and 50 rounds of machine-gun ammunition. Once this crash course was complete, the tank crews were sent to their new units.

In 1942, Soviet tank-crew training courses were frequently cut short due to urgent demands from the front, and so there were not enough tank crews trained to fill out all of the positions. So for example, in 1942 some 34,664 tank crewmen were trained, but the numbers of new tanks manufactured in 1942 required more than 82,000

A T-34 Model 1941 of the 1st Red Banner Tank Brigade in Vyborg (Finnish: Viipuri) on 20 June 1944. This tank is something of a mystery. Aside from being fitted with a German tank commander's cupola, it was the oldest known example of a T-34 in Soviet service in Finland in 1944. There is some speculation that it was a Soviet tank that was captured and modified by the Germans, then recaptured by the Red Army and put back into Soviet service in 1944.

crewmen. This forced units to fill out positions with untrained troops. The limited training of the tank crews led to complaints from the front, and the training programmes were expanded considerably in later years. By 1944, a larger percentage of the Red Army's tank crews had gone through formal crew training.

THE FINNISH ASSAULT GUN BATTALION

The Finnish Army established an Assault Gun Battalion (Ryn.Tyk.P.: *Rynnäkkötykkipataljoona*) as part of its Armoured Division (*Panssaridivisioonal*) on 15 February 1943. The battalion was initially equipped with the BT-42 assault gun, which was a Finnish conversion of captured Soviet BT-7 Model 1937 light cavalry tanks modified with an enlarged turret and armed with the British QF 4.5in Mark II howitzer. A total of 18 BT-7 were converted, with deliveries of the BT-42 assault guns starting in February 1943 and continuing until late autumn 1943. The BT-42 were first deployed along the Svir River in June 1943; but though they proved very effective in destroying bunkers and strongpoints, the 4.5in howitzer they mounted was not well suited to destroying tanks.

The Finnish Armoured Division was equipped primarily with captured Soviet tanks consisting mainly of T-26 light tanks, plus small numbers of T-34 medium and KV-1 heavy tanks. In 1943, Finland approached Germany regarding a possible purchase of more modern equipment. The initial plan was to acquire 45 StuG III which were viewed as an economical but combat-effective option. As a result, Germany agreed to provide training for a cadre of Finnish Army crewmen who could then train the remainder of the Assault Gun Battalion. After the 30 StuG III arrived, the BT-42 assault guns were shuffled off to a Detached Armour Company (Er.Ps.K.: *Erilliselle Pansaarikompanialle*) which was formed in December 1943.

A Finnish cadre of three officers, 14 NCOs and 22 men arrived in Germany in late June 1943 and were sent to the Adolf Hitler Lager near Jüterborg to attend the Sturmartillerieschule. This was a five-week course, with a portion of the Finnish troops learning to operate the StuG III while about half the Finns were assigned to a special technical course on maintaining and repairing the vehicle. The Finns were quite pleased with the high technical standards of the training and the initial cadre returned to Finland in early August 1943 to begin training the remainder of the Assault Gun Battalion. A second technical cadre was sent to Magdeburg in Germany in mid-November 1943 for additional maintenance training. In addition, a small German technical cadre was sent to Finland to provide further instruction.

Delivery of the 30 StuG III from Germany took place in the summer of 1943, with the first batch of ten arriving on 6 July, eight more on 10 August and the final batch of 12 on 3 September. Ammunition allotments for training were not generous, consisting of 200 armour-piercing (AP) and 300 high-explosive (HE) rounds, and only 54 rounds were actually used. Major Eric Åkerman was appointed to lead the Assault Gun Battalion after receiving special training in Germany. Several of the Finnish officers serving in the battalion were experienced

OVERLEAF

Sturmi Ps. 531-10 'Bubi' followed by Ps. 531-11 'Airi' during the 4 June 1944 parade at Enso (now Svetogorsk). 'Bubi' was commanded by Staff Sergeant Börje Brotell with gunner Lance Corporal Olli Soimala and was the highest-scoring Sturmi of the campaign, credited with 11 Soviet tanks and assault guns. (SA-kuva)

combat veterans who had served with the Finnish Waffen-SS detachment on the Eastern Front in 1942–43, but most were recruited out of the Finnish Army's artillery branch.

The Assault Gun Battalion was equipped with standard German tracked vehicles and half-tracks which were delivered in early 1944. The nominal table of organization for the battalion was 310 men. Four StuG III used during training were diverted to an artillery depot as a battalion reserve, followed by four more prior to the start of the summer 1944 fighting. The supply of spare parts with the StuG III deliveries had not been generous and as a result, another StuG III was set aside later for potential cannibalization for spares. The Assault Gun Battalion was organized into three companies. Each company consisted of a headquarters with two assault guns and three batteries, each with three assault guns for a total of 11. On paper, the battalion had 34 assault guns: one battalion HQ assault gun plus three companies with 11 assault guns each because Finland had planned to acquire 45 assault guns in total. Actual strength at the start of the summer fighting was 22 assault guns due to the diversion of a portion of the fleet to reserve/depot status.

Once delivered, the Finnish StuG III were sent to the Tank Centre (Panssarikeskus) in Varkaus for various modifications. As mentioned earlier, the *Schürzen* side skirts were removed. The secondary armament of the vehicles was modified with captured Soviet DT machine guns substituted for the usual MG 42 over the loader's hatch and Suomi submachine guns replacing the German MP 40s for crew self-defence. The spare road wheels were moved from the engine deck to the superstructure side to provide space for a large wooden storage bin mounted on the rear hull. All of the vehicles were repainted in Finnish three-tone camouflage along with Hakaristi (swastika) national markings. Finnish armoured vehicles received a standardized registration number in the pattern of Ps 531-X, with the 'Ps' indicating Panssari (armour), '531' indicating the StuG III, and the final number a sequential series running from 1 to 30.

The first assault gun used by the Finnish Army was the BT-42 conversion consisting of a captured Soviet BT-7 Model 1937 light tank fitted with a British QF 4.5in Mark II howitzer in a heavily modified turret. The Assault Gun Battalion used BT-42s until it started receiving the first batch of Sturmis in September 1943. The BT-42s were transferred to a new Detached Armour Company which fought in the battle for Vyborg on 20 June 1944 where this example, R-717, was knocked out.

MAURI SARTIO

Mauri Sartio was born in August 1916 in Viipuri, then part of Imperial Russia. He served in the Finnish Army in the 1939–40 Winter War. In early 1941, the Finnish government began recruiting experienced Finnish soldiers for service in a Finnish volunteer unit for the German Waffen-SS. Sartio volunteered and arrived in Germany in late May 1941. The Finnisches Freiwilligen-Bataillon der Waffen-SS (FFB-WSS) was a motorized infantry battalion, attached to SS-Regiment *Nordland* of the SS Division *Wiking*. This battalion was initially deployed in January 1942 and saw combat in the Caucasus in mid-1942 and in the Third Battle of Kharkov in early 1943. Satio eventually led the 2nd Company of the FFB-WSS in March-July 1943 while holding the rank of *SS-Obersturmführer* (captain). While in German service, Sartio was awarded the Iron Cross 1st Class and 2nd Class, the Ost Medaille and the Infantry Assault Badge. The FFB-WSS was disbanded in mid-1943 after the two-year enlistment period expired, and the Finnish government declined to support the effort any further. As a result, Sartio returned to the Finnish Army as a captain and was eventually assigned to the Assault Gun Battalion, due to his experience as well as his German-language skills. At the start of the summer 1944 campaign, he led a platoon of the 1st Company, Assault Gun Battalion. He commanded Sturmi Ps. 531-19 'Marjatta'; his gunner originally was Lance Corporal Olof Lagus, the son of the Finnish Armoured Division commander, Major General Ernst Ruben Lagus. Sartio's assault gun led the counter-attack into Kuuterselkä on 14 June 1944, knocking out four T-34 tanks in the initial skirmish. His Sturmi was subsequently credited with another two T-34 kills at Portinhoikka on 25 June and another tank on a subsequent date; these later victories were credited to his new gunner, Corporal Reino Antilla. Sartio survived the war and died in March 1986.

Captain Mauri Sartio, 9 July 1944. (SA-kuva)

By the time of the Soviet 1944 summer offensive, the Assault Gun Battalion had had ample time for training. It is difficult to compare the level of training to that of their opposing Red Army tank crews, but it was more extensive than that offered to the average Soviet tank crewman.

Besides the Finnish Assault Gun Battalion, two German StuG units also fought in Karelia in the summer of 1944. Sturmgeschütz-Brigade 303 was sent as reinforcements after the initial Soviet offensive and fought alongside the Finnish Assault Gun Battalion during the battle of Tali-Ihantala in late June and early July 1944. Sturmgeschütz-Abteilung 1122 was a *Sturmgeschütz* unit subordinated to 122. Infanterie-Division that took part in the fighting at the Bay of Vyborg from 30 June to 2 August 1944.

THE STRATEGIC SITUATION

Following the summer 1941 campaign to regain Karelia and other territory captured by the Soviet Union during the Winter War of November 1939–March 1940, the Finnish Army halted any further Red Army advance towards Leningrad. In late September 1941, Finland informed the Oberkommando des Heeres (OKH: High Command of the German Army) that the Finnish Army would not push any further south beyond the Svir River or its current positions in the Karelian Isthmus. In November 1941, the Finnish Army in Karelia began establishing a secondary defensive line from Vammelsuu (now Serovo) on the Gulf of Finland to Taipale on Lake Ladoga, called the VT Line. The Finnish Army began demobilizing troops in December 1941 from the older age groups, with the result that numbers declined from 460,000 to 350,000 men by the autumn of 1942. The German Army deployed forces in Finland that attempted to cut off the critical Soviet ports around Arkhangel in the far north, but they received tepid support from the Finns for this effort and failed to secure this objective. The Finnish–Soviet front in Karelia remained in a state of deliberate stalemate for two years.

By February 1944, the Red Army had lifted the German siege of Leningrad and began to push westward along the Baltic coast towards East Prussia. It soon became evident to the Finnish government in Helsinki that the Red Army would eventually start a campaign to knock Finland out of the war. The first stage of that effort began with three massive but mostly ineffective bombardments of Helsinki in February 1944. Because the areas north of Leningrad were now free from German troops, the Red Army could begin to mass troops at the southern end of the Karelian Isthmus

Much of the terrain on the Karelian Isthmus comprised numerous swamps, bogs and forests which hindered large-scale tank operations. This is a scene in front of the strongpoints of the Finnish 10th Company, 57th Infantry Regiment near Vuosalmi after the fighting in early September 1944. The area has been completely devastated by Soviet artillery and the wreck of a T-34 Model 1943 of the 222nd Separate Tank Regiment can be seen in the middle distance. (SA-kuva)

facing Finland. As a result, the Finnish government began attempts to withdraw from the conflict.

An American-sponsored initiative led to discussions with Soviet representatives in Stockholm about peace terms. The Soviet government demanded a return to the 1940 borders, and also added a new demand that German troops on Finnish soil should be interned for the duration of the war. The Finnish parliament was not willing to accept these terms without further discussion and a delegation departed for Moscow in late March 1944. The situation seemed all the more ominous because Hungary was occupied by German troops on 20 March 1944 after having started preliminary talks about peace negotiations with the Soviet Union. One day later, on 21 March, the same action occurred in Romania. Finland was not as vulnerable as Hungary and Romania because the German forces were concentrated in the arctic north, not in the populated south, and they were not strong enough in numbers to overcome the Finnish Army. On returning to Finland, the Moscow delegation revealed that Stalin insisted that the Germans be interned or driven out by the end of April and that Finland agree to an indemnity of $600 million over the next five years. The Finnish government thought that the terms were impossible and rejected them on 18 April 1944. Helsinki hoped that Moscow would simply ignore Finland for the time being, assessing that it posed no threat. Stalin felt otherwise.

Stalin ordered a brief and decisive two-phase assault on Finland to start in early June 1944. Marshal Leonid A. Govorov's Leningrad Front was ordered to initiate the campaign by striking along the Gulf of Finland on the Baltic coast towards Vyborg with the aim of securing the city in ten days. This would be followed by the Svir–

Petrozavodsk campaign by General Kirill A. Meretskov's Karelian Front, advancing north of Lake Ladoga.

In light of the embarrassing performance of the Red Army in the Winter War, preparations for this operation were both thorough and precise. Owing to the enormous loss of manpower in 1941–44, the Red Army intended to rely on its overwhelming advantages in firepower. The Leningrad Front deployed two field armies on this campaign: General Lieutenant Dmitrii N. Gusev's 21st Combined Arms Army on the left flank along the Baltic coast and General Lieutenant Aleksandr I. Cherepanov's 23rd Combined Arms Army on the right flank along the western shores of Lake Ladoga. Air support was provided by the 13th Air Army. Owing to the extensive use of fortifications by the Finnish Army, the 21st Combined Arms Army had an unusually heavy concentration of artillery including two artillery breakthrough divisions, a gun artillery brigade, five high-power artillery divisions and seven self-propelled artillery regiments. Soviet forces in this phase of the campaign involved about 260,000 men, 5,500 guns and mortars, 880 Katyusha multiple rocket launchers, 628 tanks and self-propelled guns and 700 combat aircraft. The ratio of Soviet forces arrayed against the Finns included a 2.6:1 advantage in manpower, 6:1 advantage in artillery, and 6:1 advantage in tanks.

The Finnish Army continued to rely on fortified defensive lines as a means to enhance the defensive capabilities of its badly outnumbered infantry. In 1944, the VT Line was reinforced by the Viipuri–Kuparsaari–Taipale (VKT) Line on the northern side of the Karelian Isthmus in conjunction with the Uuksu (U) Line in the Sortavala sector. The 1944 defensive lines were different to the Mannerheim Line that saw the focus of fighting in 1939–40. The new lines relied on trenches studded with log-reinforced strongpoints and concrete bunkers. On average, each kilometre of a defensive line contained 28–32 machine-gun and light mortar nests, 9–12 log strongpoints and 6–9 bunkers.

The focus of this account is on the sector along the Gulf of Finland that initially pitted the Soviet 21st Combined Arms Army against the Finnish Army's 10th Infantry Division. The 21st Combined Arms Army consisted of five rifle corps although only three were used in the initial phase (as detailed in the accompanying chart). Each rifle corps consisted of three rifle divisions for a total of 15 divisions in this sector. While this might seem like a massive force, it should be noted that Red Army rifle divisions at this stage of the war were usually understrength, with 3,000–4,000 men, and that the typical rifle corps was closer in size to a British or American infantry division.

The Finnish Army in this sector included elements of Lieutenant General Hjalmar Siilasvuo's 3rd Corps to the north-east and Lieutenant General Taavetti Laatikainen's 4th Corps along the Gulf of Finland to the south-west. The initial line of defence, called the Main Position, was defended by the 15th, 2nd and 10th Infantry divisions as well as the 19th Infantry Brigade. The second echelon consisted of the 3rd and 18th

21st Combined Arms Army (General Lieutenant Dmitrii N. Gusev)

30th Guards Rifle Corps (General Lieutenant N.P. Simonyak): 45th, 63rd and 64th Guards Rifle divisions

97th Rifle Corps (General Major M.M. Busarov): 178th, 358th and 381st Rifle divisions

109th Rifle Corps (General Lieutenant I.P. Alferov): 72nd, 109th and 286th Rifle divisions

Work on the VT Line was accelerated in the late spring of 1944 as the threat of a Soviet offensive increased. This is part of the anti-tank obstacle belt near Kuuterselkä. The stone obstacles were placed snugly to prevent tanks being able to knock them over, while at the same time the obstacles were high enough to catch the belly of any tank that tried to pass over them. (SA-kuva)

Infantry divisions and the Cavalry Brigade. The Finnish Armoured Division was the operational reserve for this sector and included the Assault Gun Battalion.

The Red Army launched its offensive against Finland at 0700hrs Finnish time (the Red Army used Moscow time, which was one hour later) on 9 June 1944, beginning with air attacks on the Finnish defence lines. There was an initial five-minute barrage by all artillery weapons, followed by ten hours of artillery fire against specific targets. The artillery fire that day totalled 76,583 rounds. Vigorous reconnaissance probes penetrated the Finnish defence line in two locations. At Mottori in the Valkeasaari area, the reconnaissance attack included ten obsolete T-26 light tanks of the 220th Tank Brigade, all of which were knocked out during the probe.

The main ground attack began at 0500hrs on 10 June after a 40-minute artillery preparation. The Soviet 21st Combined Arms Army fired 192,690 rounds of artillery during the day. The ferocity of the attack and the substantial Soviet advantage in manpower, tanks and artillery was overwhelming. The attack hit the defences of the Finnish 10th Infantry Division which by the end of the day had suffered substantial losses. The defence line was penetrated in numerous locations and the 10th Infantry Division had to be withdrawn on 11 June because it was no longer combat-effective. The Soviet offensive forced the Finnish Army to begin shifting forces into this sector.

On 11 June, Govorov's 21st Combined Arms Army reconfigured its tank forces to exploit the breakthrough achieved on the first day of the attack. The supporting tank units were united into battle groups to assist the two corps. Group No. 1, consisting of the 152nd Tank Brigade and the 26th Guards Heavy Tank Regiment (IS-2), spearheaded the 109th Rifle Corps. Group No. 2, consisting of the 1st Red Banner Tank Brigade and the 27th Guards Heavy Tank Regiment (IS-2), spearheaded the 30th Guards Rifle Corps. The Finnish defences were cracked open and a number of Finnish units were routed. On 11 June, elements of the 30th Guards Rifle Corps and 109th Rifle Corps advanced about 15km.

The Finnish Armoured Division counter-attacked with two of its *Jäger* (light infantry) battalions (Jääkräi Pataljoona 2 and Jääkräi Pataljoona 5) and two anti-tank companies from its anti-tank battalion. During the counter-attack from Kivennapa towards Polviselkä on 11 June, the anti-tank companies destroyed 17 Red Army tanks with their 7.5cm PaK 40 guns. Eight of these losses were from the 31st Guards Separate Heavy Breakthrough Tank Regiment and the remainder from the 152nd Tank Brigade. However, the Finnish force was obliged to retreat behind the VT Line.

By the end of 11 June, reinforcements from the Finnish 3rd Infantry Division arrived and took up positions on the VT Line. The Cavalry Brigade took over the VT Line closest to the Gulf of Finland, and the shattered 10th Infantry Division withdrew through the VT Line. Further to the east, the 2nd Infantry Division moved into the VT Line along with the 18th Infantry Division on its left flank.

The Finnish infantry divisions had a great deal of difficulty defending against Soviet tanks. Anti-tank weapons that had been effective in the 1941 campaign had become obsolete in the intervening years. In 1941, the Red Army tank force on the Finnish front consisted mainly of light tanks such as the T-26 and BT-7, but by 1944 this had shifted to the more heavily armoured T-34 medium tank and KV/IS heavy tanks. The most numerous Finnish anti-tank weapon was the 20mm Lahti anti-tank rifle. A total of 1,789 L-39 anti-tank rifles were in service on 1 June 1944, but they were ineffective against the frontal armour of Soviet medium and heavy tanks and older anti-tank guns in the 37–45mm range were little better. The most widely used anti-tank gun in Finnish service was the Soviet 45mm gun in various sub-variants. There were 670 of these weapons in service in 1944 and they were used for infantry defence at regimental and battalion level. Finland imported small numbers of German anti-tank guns in 1942–43 including 27 5cm PaK 38 and 46 7.5cm PaK 97/38. The best of the anti-tank guns in service in 1944 were the 210 7.5cm PaK 40 purchased from Germany in 1943–44. These were usually retained in divisional-level anti-tank companies.

One of the most important additions to the Finnish arsenal were a variety of new German anti-tank rocket weapons. In April 1944, Finland received 300 8.8cm Raketenpanzerbüchse 43 *Panzerschreck* anti-tank rocket launchers. The same shipment also included 1,700 *Panzerfaust* one-shot anti-tank rocket launchers. Unfortunately, these new weapons were still in the Finnish Army depots when the Soviet offensive began. They were delivered to the troops after the fighting had started but with very little training in their use.

The pace of the Soviet offensive slowed on 12 June due to clashes with the new Finnish reinforcements. The Finns claimed to have knocked out 29 Soviet tanks that day, but the 21st Combined Arms Army nevertheless reached portions of the VT Line. The focus of the Soviet attack began to centre on Kivennapa because it sat astride the main road to Vyborg, the tactical objective of the campaign. The Finns

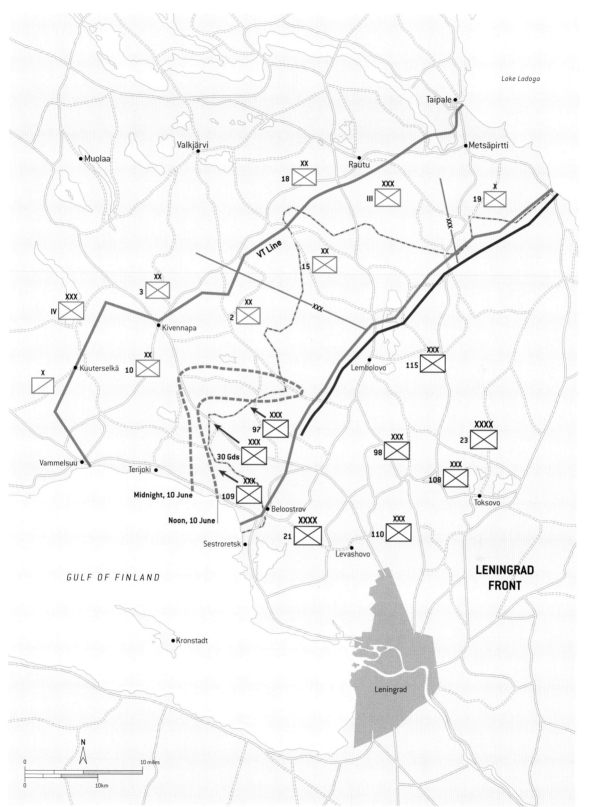

Lake Ladoga

Taipale

Metsäpirtti

Valkjärvi

Muolaa

Rautu

XX
18

XXX
III

X
19

XXX

VT Line

XX
15

XX
3

XXX
IV

XX
2

Kivennapa

XXX

X

Kuuterselkä

XX
10

Lembolovo

XXX
115

XXX
97

XXXX
23

XXX
30 Gds

XXX
98

Vammelsuu

Terijoki

Midnight, 10 June

XXX
109

Noon, 10 June

Beloostrov

XXX
108

Toksovo

XXXX
21

XXX
110

Sestroretsk

Levashovo

**LENINGRAD
FRONT**

GULF OF FINLAND

Kronstadt

N

0   10 miles
0   10km

Leningrad

The Finnish Army obtained modest supplies of new German anti-tank weapons prior to the summer 1944 campaign. Here, Finnish troops of JR 11 examine the new German weapons on 19 June 1944 at an ammunition distribution point, including a *Panzerschreck* anti-tank rocket launcher in the foreground and a *Panzerfaust* one-shot anti-tank rocket launcher in the hands of the soldier in the centre. The distribution of these weapons from the depots was delayed in the spring of 1944 for administrative reasons and the troops fought for the first days of the summer 1944 campaign without these very effective weapons. (SA-kuva)

realized that this was the most likely objective of the Soviet offensive, and so reinforced this sector.

The first tanks of Colonel Vasily Volkov's 1st Red Banner Tank Brigade reached the VT Line at the village of Kuuterselkä (now Lebyazhye) on the morning of 12 June, losing three T-60 light tanks in the process; two other T-60s and two T-34s were hit but not destroyed. The Soviet tanks had been taken by surprise by a single 7.5cm PaK 40. The tank attack was renewed at 1630hrs and a further T-34 and two T-60 tanks were destroyed. The Finnish gunner, Corporal Veikko Leppäkoski from the 8th Gun Company claimed six kills (three KV-1 and three T-34 tanks). Volkov's brigade withdrew for rest and replenishment.

On 13 June, the forces of the 21st Combined Arms Army took a short pause before trying to penetrate the VT Line. Govorov ordered the forward units to conduct reconnaissance-in-force along the VT Line to locate any potential weak points. These probes discovered that Kivennapa was well defended but that the neighbouring village of Kuuterselkä appeared to be more vulnerable. This set the stage for the battle of Kuuterselkä the following day, 14 June, in what would turn out to be one of the largest armoured vehicle battles of the Finnish campaign.

COMBAT

General Lieutenant Ivan P. Alferov's 109th Rifle Corps was given the assignment to break through the VT Line in the vicinity of Kuuterselkä. Its three rifle divisions were deployed, left to right, 109th Rifle Division, 286th Rifle Division and 72nd Rifle Division. The 109th Rifle Division, advancing on the left flank along the railway line, was supported by the 1st Red Banner Tank Brigade. On the morning of Wednesday, 14 June, the tank brigade had 26 T-34 and ten T-60/T-70 tanks still operational from a starting strength at the beginning of the offensive of 30 T-34s and 21 T-60/T-70s. The two rifle divisions in the centre and on the right flank were supported by an armoured force consisting of the 185th Separate Tank Regiment, 98th Separate Tank Regiment and the 1222nd Self-propelled Gun (SPG) Regiment. The 185th Separate Tank Regiment had about 17 operational T-34s from a starting strength of 21 tanks. The 1222nd SPG Regiment had 17 of its original 21 SU-76M self-propelled guns.

The Finnish forces at Kuuterselkä were positioned on the VT Line which ran at an angle to the main road. The initial line was held by Major Aito Keravuori's 2nd Battalion, 53rd Infantry Regiment. There was a secondary switch position that ran through Kuuterselkä. The balance of forces clearly favoured the Red Army: a single Finnish infantry battalion in partially completed defences faced two Soviet divisions with tank support.

The Red Army force for the attack on Kuuterselkä consisted of the 286th Rifle Division on the western side of the main road and the 72nd Rifle Division to the east of the road. The armoured support was mainly in front of the 72nd Rifle Division. The attack was preceded by a company of sappers to deal with mines and other obstacles, followed by the 98th Separate Tank Regiment, 185th Separate Tank Regiment, 1222nd SPG Regiment, Lieutenant Colonel Vasili I. Korolev's 14th Rifle Regiment and Major Koliuch's 133rd Rifle Regiment from the 72nd Rifle Division and the 994th Rifle Regiment from the 286th Rifle Division.

Senior Lieutenant Vasily T. Vasiliev's T-34 No. 958 of the 185th Separate Tank Regiment enters Terijoki (now Zelenogorsk) on 11 June 1944.

The attack began at 0700hrs with a 75-minute heavy artillery preparation against the VT Line. Thick cloud cover that day prevented the use of medium bombers, so the main air support missions were conducted by Ilyushin Il-2 Sturmovik ground-attack aircraft. The Sturmoviks roamed over the VT Line for six hours, striking any identifiable target.

Once the artillery fire lifted at 0830hrs, the 286th Rifle Division advanced on the left flank with its 994th Rifle Regiment as its spearhead, supported by the 98th Separate Tank Regiment. By 0945hrs the 286th Rifle Division had penetrated the VT Line in many places and continued advancing to Kuuterselkä, which it captured by 1200hrs. On the right flank, the 72nd Rifle Division with its 133rd Rifle Regiment in the front was supported by the 185th Separate Tank Regiment and parts of the 1222nd SPG Regiment. These units also began their advance at about 0830hrs. The Red Army infantry took heavy losses, but eventually, one of the tank company commanders, Senior Lieutenant Vasily T. Vasiliev, managed to manoeuvre his T-34 (No. 958) through a gap in the barbed wire and tank obstacle belts at about 1300hrs, opening up a gap in the VT Line in their sector.

At 0810hrs, the 3rd Division commander, Lieutenant General Aaro Pajari, ordered the 1st Battalion, 48th Infantry Regiment to move forward to assist in the defence of the VT Line. However, by 0945hrs, Soviet infantry already had penetrated the VT Line at several points. The Finnish bunkers continued to pour machine-gun fire against the exposed Soviet infantry, and eventually the 72nd Rifle Division moved up some of its 57mm ZiS-2 anti-tank guns to eliminate the bunkers by firing directly against their embrasures.

Major Keravuori's 2nd Battalion, 53rd Infantry Regiment was forced to retreat later in the morning and attempted to re-establish its defences in the switch line in Kuuterselkä. By 1230hrs, the 1st Battalion, 48th Infantry Regiment had arrived along the switch line. By the early afternoon, the momentum of the battle favoured the Soviet attack and the switch line through Kuuterselkä was overcome by the 133rd Rifle

OPPOSITE

The battle of Kuuterselkä, 14–15 June 1944.

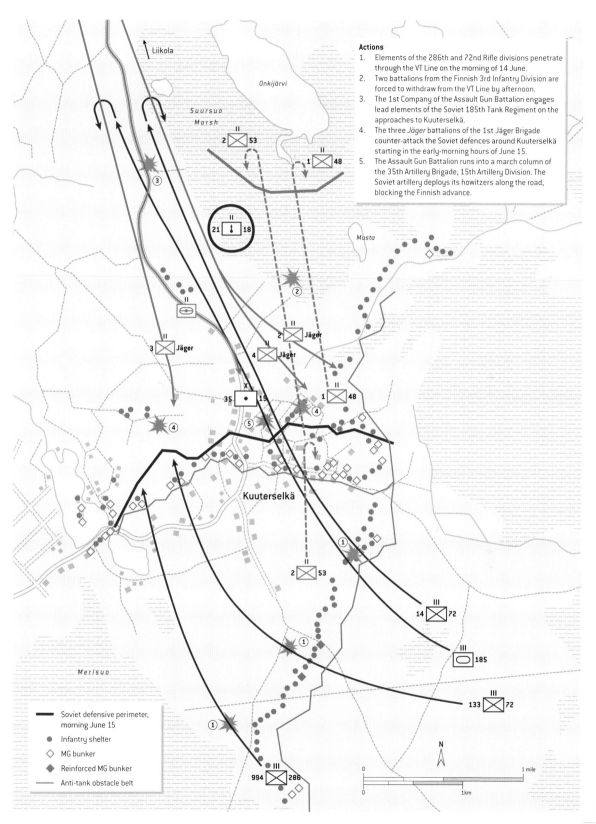

Liikola

Onkijärvi

Suursuo
Marsh

Musta

Actions

1. Elements of the 286th and 72nd Rifle divisions penetrate through the VT Line on the morning of 14 June.
2. Two battalions from the Finnish 3rd Infantry Division are forced to withdraw from the VT Line by afternoon.
3. The 1st Company of the Assault Gun Battalion engages lead elements of the Soviet 185th Tank Regiment on the approaches to Kuuterselkä.
4. The three *Jäger* battalions of the 1st Jäger Brigade counter-attack the Soviet defences around Kuuterselkä starting in the early-morning hours of June 15.
5. The Assault Gun Battalion runs into a march column of the 35th Artillery Brigade, 15th Artillery Division. The Soviet artillery deploys its howitzers along the road, blocking the Finnish advance.

2 | 53

1 | 48

21 | 18

3

2

3 | Jäger

2 | Jäger

4 | Jäger

35 | 15

1 | 48

4

5

4

Kuuterselkä

1

2 | 53

1

14 | 72

1

185

1

133 | 72

Merisuo

1

994 | 286

Soviet defensive perimeter, morning June 15

● Infantry shelter

◇ MG bunker

◆ Reinforced MG bunker

Anti-tank obstacle belt

N

0 ——— 1 mile

0 ——— 1km

A T-34 Model 1943 of Colonel Vasily Volkov's 1st Red Banner Tank Brigade in Vyborg on 20 June 1944. This tank is the later production style with the commander's cupola. The 1st Red Banner Tank Brigade fought to the west of the 185th Separate Tank Regiment at the time of the battle of Kuuterselkä.

Regiment. The Finnish 1st Battalion, 48th Infantry Regiment staged a counter-attack but was unable to dislodge the Soviet infantry.

By late afternoon, the Finnish VT Line defences were thoroughly ruptured and the forward Soviet troops had advanced north beyond Kuuterselkä, reaching to within 1.5km south of the village of Liikola on the southern shores of Lake Onkijärvi. The 3rd Division had already committed its very modest reserves, and so the Soviet penetrations along the line could not be counter-attacked. Lieutenant General Laatikainen, the 4th Corps' commander, had two options. He could order a general retreat to the next defence line, or he could scrape together a counter-attack force from units arriving in the 4th Corps' sector since the start of the Soviet offensive. He chose the latter option.

The main counter-attack force was called Taisteluosasto Puroma (Battlegroup Puroma) after its commander, Colonel Albert Puroma, a decorated infantry leader who had received the Mannerheim Cross in October 1942 for his leadership of the 12th Infantry Regiment. In February 1944, Puroma was assigned to lead the 1st Jäger Brigade, the infantry element of the Finnish Armoured Division. Battlegroup Puroma included the 1st Jäger Brigade's three *Jäger* battalions (JP 2, JP 3 and JP 4) and totalled about 3,150 men. Some of the *Jäger* battalions had already seen extensive combat in Polviselkä on 11 June. Unlike the other Finnish units in this sector, the soldiers of the 1st Jäger Brigade had received training in co-operation with tanks as well as special anti-tank training. The brigade had received the first new German-supplied *Panzerfäuste* only two days before, on 12 June.

On the afternoon of 14 June, Major Åkerman's Assault Gun Battalion, located in the Parkkila area, 2km north on Lake Suulajärvi, was subordinated to Battlegroup Puroma, but it took most of the afternoon and evening for it to reach the Kuuterselkä sector. At the time, the Assault Gun Battalion had 22 assault guns ready for combat.

Puroma's units moved south to the areas near Lake Suulajärvi and the village of Liikola. Around 1550hrs, Puroma's battlegroup received the order to immediately

Jäger light infantry of Battlegroup Puroma are shown here cycling towards Kuuterselkä on the evening of 14 June 1944 at the start of the Finnish counter-attack. (SA-kuva)

commence the counter-attack. The subsequent focus of the engagement was a narrow corridor along the Kuuterselkä–Liikola road because the area east of the road was the Suursuo marsh. On arrival south of Liikola, Åkerman met with Puroma to discuss the forthcoming attack.

The initial phase of the counter-attack was supported by 11 Junkers Ju 88 bombers of PLeLv 44 (Pommituslentolaivue: Bomber Squadron 44) that dropped 12 tonnes of bombs on Soviet troops at 1753–1800hrs. The sortie was intercepted by Soviet fighters but Finnish Messerschmitt Bf 109 fighters managed to keep them away from the bombers, scoring two aerial victories over the Soviet Bell P-39 Airacobra fighters. By 1800hrs JP 2, along with the 1st Battalion of JR 48 reached the southern end of Lake Onkijärvi and brought the Soviet forces to a halt.

Puroma set the time of the counter-attack for sunset: 2245hrs. (June is the period of 'white nights' in this northern latitude, with sunset close to midnight. The counter-attack commenced in this twilight.) Puroma was promised both artillery and air support. Another air strike, this time by 11 Bristol Blenheims from PLeLv 42 carrying 6.5 tonnes of bombs and a mixture of 11 bombers from PLeLv 46 with a further 17.5 tonnes of bombs, hit Soviet forces near Kuuterselkä at 2320–2337hrs. The Finnish artillery barrage by four artillery battalions was weak, however, due to ammunition shortages.

Soviet intelligence had received information that the Finns were going to use the Armoured Division for the counter-attack. The Soviets prepared themselves by collecting one T-34-85 company from the 98th Separate Tank Regiment, a company of five IS-2 tanks from the 27th Guards Separate Heavy Tank Regiment and the

The Finnish Assault Gun Battalion at Kuuterselkä, 14 June 1944

Unit	Commander	Vehicle Number/Name
Battalion HQ	Major Eric Åkerman	Ps. 531-23
1st Company	Captain Carl-Birger Kvikant	Ps. 531-29
2nd Company	Captain Werner von Troil	Ps. 531-1 'Aune'
3rd Company	Captain Tor Kumlin	Ps. 531-20 'Meeri'

One of the few photos of the Finnish Assault Gun Brigade in action at Kuuterselkä shows Sturmi Ps. 531-17 at the Liikola crossroads on the evening of 14 June 1944 moving towards Kuuterselkä. The counter-attack began a few hours later. (SA-kuva)

31st Guards Separate Heavy Breakthrough Tank Regiment to reinforce the 185th Separate Tank Regiment and the 1222nd SPG Regiment.

Battlegroup Puroma began its counter-attack at 2246hrs with JP 4 in the lead, supported by the 1st Company of the Assault Gun Battalion. After a hard day's fighting, the Soviet 14th Rifle Regiment had taken up defensive positions for the night to the east of the Hevossaari meadows. A tank company from the 185th Separate Tank Regiment with five T-34 and T-34-85 tanks was located on either side of the Kuuterselkä–Liikola road on a shallow hillock; their crews were preparing to get some sleep before the fighting resumed the next day. There were other Soviet forces ahead of them, and the exhausted tank company does not appear to have established perimeter guards.

The Soviet tankers were not expecting an armoured attack and were surprised when the Finnish assault guns came charging down the road. The lead Sturmi, Ps. 531-19 'Marjatta', commanded by Lieutenant Mauri Sartio, suddenly encountered a Soviet tank to its left. Sartio ordered his driver to quickly steer perpendicular to the road, aiming at a T-34 or T-34-85 barely 15m away. The Sturmi's gunner was Lance Corporal Olof Lagus, son of the Finnish Armoured Division commander, Major General Ernst Ruben Lagus. Lance Corporal Lagus took aim at the Soviet tank and knocked it out at point-blank range. Sartio's Sturmi knocked out two more T-34 tanks in the violent mêlée, while two other Soviet tanks tried to escape down the road to Kuuterselkä. One of the fleeing tanks was hit by Sartio's Sturmi while the other was hit by Sturmi Ps. 531-3 commanded by Staff Sergeant Pellervo Hyytiäinen. The Soviet tanks managed to return fire and Hyytiäinen's Sturmi was hit but not knocked out. Sartio's Sturmi had a problem with its gun's semi-automatic breech mechanism and was obliged to withdraw as well. One of the Soviet tanks knocked out in this mêlée was Vasiliev's T-34 No. 958, and he was killed in the action.

One of the minor mysteries of this engagement concerned the Soviet tank types involved. Some Finnish accounts indicate that they were T-34-85s, but Soviet accounts indicate that the unit involved was the 185th Separate Tank Regiment, which was not

Sturmi Ps. 531-17, commanded by Sergeant Eino Räsänen, was knocked out during the fighting at Kuuterselkä after having been hit by Soviet gunfire on the hull front and gun. Two of the crew, the driver and loader, were wounded. This Sturmi was gutted by fire after Räsänen set off an explosive charge inside when the crew abandoned the stricken vehicle.

known to have the T-34-85. It is likely that T-34 Model 1942s and Model 1943s with high hexagonal turrets were misidentified as the T-34-85. Another possibility is that there were some T-34-85s mixed in with the forward detachment of the 185th Separate Tank Regiment. The 98th Separate Tank Regiment, equipped with T-34-85s, was attached to the 109th Rifle Corps that day.

With Sartio's Sturmi as well as Sergeant Pertti Nertamo's Ps. 531-4 temporarily out of action, the 1st Company commander, Captain Carl-Birger Kvikant, ordered the second platoon under Lieutenant Olli Aulanko to continue in the front. After a while Aulanko's Sturmi, Ps. 531-6 'Liisa' encountered a SU-76M self-propelled assault gun, sometimes misidentified as an ISU-152. The Sturmi gunner, Corporal Olavi Taponen, knocked out the SU-76M with a single shot. Before entering the forest clearing north of Kuuterselkä, one Soviet T-34 engaged Aulanko's Sturmi, but missed. Taponen's aim was better and he set the T-34 on fire. On entering the forest clearing, Ps. 531-6 was hit in the right upper corner of the combat compartment. The loader, Sergeant Paavo Havu, was killed instantly. Havu had loaded the gun moments before being killed and as the Sturmi swung to the left, Taponen hit the opposing T-34. In view of the damage and casualties 'Liisa' was driven back to the rear.

Shortly before midnight, about the time the 1st Company of the Assault Gun Battalion had reached the Kuuterselkä forest clearing, the 3rd Company was ordered to join the battle and relieve the 1st Company. Captain Kvikant continued the advance in his Sturmi Ps. 531-29 followed by Corporal Ilmari Koskiniemi's Ps. 531-5 'Amalia' and Sergeant Eino Vartia's Ps. 531-7 'Anneli'. As the three vehicles approached Kuuterselkä, Vartia spotted a T-34 and engaged it at a range of 150m, hitting it in the engine compartment and setting it on fire. Not long after that, the gunner of Vartia's Sturmi, Corporal Lauri Leppänen, destroyed another T-34 and a KV-1.

The forward Soviet infantry unit, the 14th Rifle Regiment, had suffered very heavy losses during the day's fighting, including its commanding officer Lieutenant Colonel Korolev, and retreated in panic after being attacked by JP 4. Lieutenant Colonel

OVERLEAF
Duel at Kuuterselkä, 14 June 1944.

Georgi M. Shepelev of the 211th Mortar Regiment (120mm mortars) was about 1km south of the tank engagement, near the edge of the Suursuo marsh. The regiment belonged to the 18th Mortar Brigade of the 15th Artillery Division, supporting the 109th Rifle Corps in the offensive. Soviet infantry began retreating near Shepelev's positions. He ordered his unit to take up a defensive position on the south-western edge of the Suursuo marsh, where they were soon joined by two retreating T-34s as well as some anti-tank guns. The regiment managed to maintain an isolated 'hedgehog' defence of its positions for most of the morning as the Finnish infantry and assault guns advanced past them on their way towards Kuuterselkä. Shepelev's regiment attempted three counter-attacks against the Finnish infantry, but all three were beaten back. Shepelev was subsequently awarded the Hero of the Soviet Union decoration for his actions that day.

The lead elements of JP 4 and the 1st Company of the Assault Gun Battalion reached the northern edge of Kuuterselkä at about 0030hrs on Thursday, 15 June. Two of the Sturmi simultaneously engaged an unidentified Soviet tank, setting it on fire. (Although initially identified as a KV-1, the assault-gun crews later indicated it was one of the new IS-2 heavy tanks, a type not previously encountered.) When the forward Sturmis reached the Launiainen cow barn, a Soviet T-34 on the left side of the road fired at them; it was knocked out along with a SU-76M behind it. Vartia's Sturmi Ps. 531-7, the first to reach Kuuterselkä, took a high-explosive hit from a T-34 about 300m away, wounding both Vartia and his loader, Lauri Makkonen. Kvikant's Sturmi Ps. 531-29 knocked out a T-34 and a truck, but suffered problems with the gun elevation after the barrel smashed into the side of a ditch. This Sturmi was hit by a T-34 near the Launiainen cow barn.

On reaching Kuuterselkä, the assault guns came under fire from Soviet 45mm anti-tank guns of the 119th Anti-tank Battalion and the 9th Artillery Regiment, both from the 72nd Rifle Division. After about 30 minutes of fighting around

This Sturmi, Ps. 531-24, commanded by Sergeant Erkki Halonen, was part of the 3rd Company of the Assault Gun Battalion. During the Finnish counter-attack, it advanced the furthest, reaching the VT Line before becoming stuck on a heap of earth. The crew threw a hand grenade into the fighting compartment and abandoned the vehicle.

Sturmi Ps. 531-5 'Amalia' was commanded at Kuuterselkä by Corporal Ilmari Koskiniemi with gunner Corporal Olavi Taponen. This Sturmi was credited with three T-34 tanks and one ISU-152 assault gun at Kuuterselkä. It is shown here on 23 June 1944 near Tienhaara on the approaches to Vyborg. It was knocked out at Vuosalmi on 11 July 1944. (SA-kuva)

Kuuterselkä, Kvikant's 1st Company of the Assault Gun Brigade was down to a single operational Sturmi, with the remaining vehicles damaged. Captain Tor Kumlin's 3rd Company was sent into action to relieve the 1st Company's assault guns, followed later by four Sturmi from Captain Werner von Troil's 2nd Company. One of the Soviet gun commanders, Junior Sergeant Boris G. Sorokin, was later awarded the Hero of the Soviet Union decoration for his actions against the Finnish assault guns that day.

On the hill approaching Kuuterselkä, the advancing Finnish assault guns were startled to see a large column of towed artillery sitting on the road. The column consisted of three artillery regiments of the 35th Artillery Brigade, 15th Artillery Division moving forward to new firing positions for planned operations later in the day. The units were unaware of the Finnish counter-attack and were in administrative march order. A wild mêlée ensued as the assault guns began firing into the stationary Soviet column. Some of the assault guns charged into the midst of the column, crushing the Soviet howitzers by driving over their trails. Senior Sergeant Boris Ya. Mamutin of the 558th Howitzer Artillery Regiment had the sense to unlimber his 122mm howitzer and deploy it against the advancing assault guns. Mamutin was subsequently credited with knocking out the lead Finnish Sturmi. Following Mamutin's example, a second crew of the battery deployed its howitzer, and eventually the entire battery under Lieutenant Aleksey Benevolenskiy was deployed for action. In the meantime, the artillery regiments further towards the tail of the column began deploying their howitzers on either side of the road in the area south of Kuuterselkä. This created a concentrated mass of firepower that eventually halted the advance of the Finnish assault guns after 0300hrs. Mamutin and Benevolenskiy were later awarded the Hero of the Soviet Union decoration for their heroism that day. A PTRD anti-tank rifleman, Mikhail G. Rusanov, of the scout platoon of the 667th Howitzer

TMFD-7 TELESCOPIC SIGHT

The reticle in the T-34's TMFD-7 telescopic sight had a 2.5× magnification with a field of view of 14°30'. There were three range scales; the left scale was marked 'SG' and the centre scale was marked 'DG' in Cyrillic. These marks were an archaic reference to old-pattern 3in blunt projectiles (SG: *staraya granata*) and streamlined projectiles (DG: *dalnoboynaya granata*), with the left column used for high explosive and the centre scale used for armour piercing. The unmarked right scale was for the machine gun. On later reticles, these columns were updated to 'O' (*oskolochnaya*: HE), 'B' (*bronebonaya*: AP) and 'P' (*pulemet*: MG). The gunner elevated the gun using the hand wheel, moving the horizontal line so that it corresponded to the target's range in metres on the respective scale. There was also a deflection scale above the range scales to compensate for crosswind from 0 to 32 in mils.

Sfl.ZF1a PERISCOPIC SIGHT

The 7.5cm StuK 40 gun on the StuG III Ausf G was aimed using the Selbstfahrlafetten Zielfernrohr Sfl.ZF1a gunner's periscopic sight which provided 5× magnification with an 8-degree field of view. The reticle consisted of an aiming chevron in the centre, with smaller triangles on either side. The gunner placed the target at the apex of the chevron. This reticle provided a limited stadiametric ranging capability which allowed a well-trained gunner to estimate the range based on the size of the target compared to the large triangle. The unit of measurement was a graduation (*strich*) equalling 1m at 1,000m range, with the triangles having sides of 2 graduations. Such calculations were too difficult in the heat of battle, so the gunner had to be so well trained that the procedure became instinctive. The series of triangles was intended to provide the gunner with a method to gauge the speed of a crossing target.

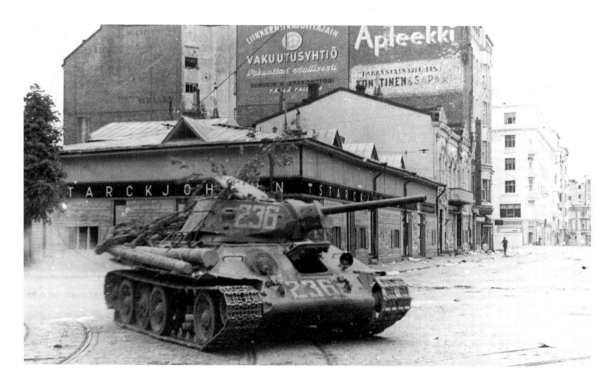

A T-34 of the 152nd Tank Brigade in Vyborg on 20 June 1944. The narrow cast turret remained in production at Factory No. 112 in Krasnoe Sormovo through the spring of 1943, and this tank is an example of that type. The tank is missing the second road wheel and the track is partly damaged.

Artillery Regiment, 15th Artillery Division was credited with knocking out another of the Finnish assault guns in this fighting, and was also awarded the Hero of the Soviet Union decoration. (There are no Finnish records that indicate any assault guns were knocked out by Soviet anti-tank rifles, though Rusanov may very well have damaged one.)

At 0244hrs on 15 June, the 3rd Company of the Finnish Assault Gun Battalion arrived in the vicinity of Launiainen cow barn, ready for action. Prior to their arrival, the 1st Company had managed to evacuate Ps. 531-7 for repair and cannibalized some parts and the radios from Ps. 531-29. Captain Kumlin started the 3rd Company attack at 0300hrs, and it would appear that all the Finnish losses in Kuuterselkä that morning were the result of hits by Soviet artillery fire. After travelling down the road a further 300m, Lieutenant Martti Myllymaa's Ps. 531-15 was hit by an anti-tank gun in the left upper corner of the fighting compartment, killing Myllymaa. The rest of the crew brought the assault gun and the body of their commander back to the rear. Soon after Ps. 531-15 was hit, Sergeant Eino Räsänen's Ps. 531-17 was hit twice by gunfire. The crew abandoned the assault gun and Räsänen set off an explosive charge inside the vehicle to scuttle it.

When leaving the Launiainen cow barn at about 0930hrs, Major Åkerman's Sturmi Ps. 531-23 was brought under fire. Åkerman was not commanding the Sturmi when a near miss by a heavy artillery round convinced the crew, mistakenly, that they had been hit and they abandoned their vehicle. Photographs taken by the Soviets after the battle show a damaged assault gun, but it is unclear whether this damage was as a result of the near miss or a subsequent hit. At 1045hrs, two Sturmi, Captain Werner von Troil's Ps. 531-1 'Aune' and Staff Sergeant Börje Brotell's Ps. 531-10 'Bubi', were operating around the Kuuterselkä forest clearing, near the cow barn on the eastern side of the road. Captain von Troil, commander of the 2nd Company, was wounded severely in the head by Soviet artillery shrapnel while away from his vehicle. Lieutenant Aulanko and Staff Sergeant Liimatta were wounded and Sergeant Havu killed by that same detonation. While first-aid was being administered at the site, another round ripped off the suspension of von Troil's assault gun. The crew abandoned the vehicle and subsequently it was set on fire by Finnish sappers.

The attack by JP 4 and the Assault Gun Battalion reached the outer fringes of the VT Line. Around 0440hrs, Sergeant Erkki Halonen's Sturmi Ps. 531-24 advanced to the western side of the Kuuterselkä hill, further than any other assault gun of the unit. In a final duel, Ps. 531-24 destroyed one T-34 and one KV-1. The crew of Ps. 531-24 never received the withdrawal order, however, and the assault gun became stuck on a heap of earth. The crew threw a hand grenade into the fighting compartment and abandoned the vehicle. This was the fifth and last Finnish assault gun lost that day.

By early morning, it was evident that the counter-attack by Battlegroup Puroma had failed to recapture the VT Line and that it would be only a matter of time before Red Army forces counter-attacked in force. Major General Lagus, the Armoured Division commander, proposed a withdrawal and Lieutenant General Laatikainen halted the counter-attack at 0700hrs on 15 June. At 1050hrs the order was given to withdraw the Armoured Division from the area. Orders were sent to the surviving assault guns, and the Assault Gun Battalion gradually filtered back north alongside the *Jäger* battalions in the afternoon.

Casualties at the battle of Kuuterselkä were high on both sides. Battlegroup Puroma suffered 627 casualties (79 KIA, 466 WIA, 82 MIA). The Soviet 72nd Rifle Division suffered 1,404 casualties during 14–15 June (179 KIA, 879 WIA and 346 MIA). These totals do not include the losses of the original two Finnish Army battalions involved in the battle, nor those suffered by the numerous Soviet units supporting the 72nd Rifle Division.

The new T-34-85 tanks were a prize capture for Finnish troops and were quickly put back into service. This T-34-85 near Pihkalanjärvi (now Druzhnoselye) on 7 July 1944 has already been repainted in Finnish three-tone camouflage colours of moss green, grey and sand brown. The Hakaristi (swastika) national marking was applied taller than the regulation size, presumably in an attempt to avoid mistaken identification. (SA-kuva)

ANALYSIS

The terrain on the Karelian Isthmus was far from ideal for large mechanized operations, with much of the area covered with boreal forests. The northern part of the isthmus is covered with marshes and further obstructed in some areas with rocky terrain. The southern part is drier with some low hills, and so is suitable for farming. The numerous lakes and rivers proved to be natural obstacles, especially when all the bridges were destroyed. There were only three main roads and two railways along the attack axis from Leningrad towards Vyborg.

The Red Army used its armoured forces in the Vyborg operation primarily for direct fire support of its rifle divisions. Arguably, Soviet artillery was a far more crucial ingredient in the eventual Soviet operational success than its armoured force. The Soviet 109th Rifle Corps succeeded in overcoming the Finnish defences of the VT Line on the approaches to Vyborg by successfully applying overwhelming force against a weak point in the Finnish defences at Kuuterselkä. Finnish units claimed to have knocked out about 40 Soviet tanks and AFVs in the battle of Kuuterselkä, about half of which were credited to the Assault Gun Battalion. Although Soviet armour units may have suffered disproportionate losses to the Assault Gun Battalion, this had no consequence in the outcome of the battle.

The Leningrad Front was able to maintain a relatively constant number of AFVs in the field from the start of the offensive to its conclusion. At the beginning of June 1944, the Leningrad Front had over 600 AFVs of which about 160 were committed in the initial battles. The strength of the force fluctuated during the campaign, reaching a peak of about 300 AFVs on 26 June, and gradually declining in early July due to attrition. An adequate supply of replacement tanks and assault guns as well as the performance of field repair units provided the Leningrad Front with continual armoured support for the duration of the campaign, in spite of combat attrition.

During the fighting near Ihantala on 30 June 1944, a single T-34 Model 1942 of the 30th Guards Tank Brigade managed to penetrate the Finnish defences. The tank was hit once by a StuG III of Sturmgeschütz-Brigade 303 commanded by Unteroffizier (Corporal) Willy Obeldobel and almost simultaneously by a *Panzerfaust* anti-tank rocket. The fuel cells in the tank exploded, blowing apart the tank. The tank commander, Junior Lieutenant Nikolay Trofimovich Zhirnov, managed to escape the conflagration but was killed by nearby Finnish infantry. (SA-kuva)

A Finnish assessment of the battle of Kuuterselkä considered Soviet advantages in troop strength and equipment to have been the essential ingredient in the Soviet victory, along with the excellent performance of Soviet artillery. However, the performance of Soviet armoured forces was not as well regarded because the numerous separate regiments operated largely without coordination, either at the operational level or tactical level. Soviet AFVs tended to approach Finnish defences very cautiously, fire on their targets and then withdraw. Inherent shortcomings in Soviet AFV design as well as the unsuitability of the Finnish terrain for tank operations contributed to this hesitant operating pattern.

The Finnish Assault Gun Battalion tended to operate in a more aggressive fashion. This was due to the presence of a significant number of experienced combat veterans as well as a greater familiarity with fighting in the local terrain conditions. The Finns tended to have greater situational awareness of the battlefield due to the better provisions for sighting equipment and radios on the StuG III. Combat tended to take place at short ranges, from as little as 15m to about 700m. Finnish casualties included five StuG III destroyed or abandoned, three StuG III damaged by enemy action, five crewmen killed and 20 wounded; about one-quarter of the StuG III force in an engagement lasting only about half a day.

During the battle for Kuuterselkä, the Finnish Assault Gun Battalion claimed to have destroyed 21 Soviet AFVs consisting of 16 T-34, three ISU-152 and two KV-1 or IS-2 heavy tanks. The Assault Gun Battalion expended 830 rounds of ammunition (470 AP, 360 HE), virtually the entire on-board supply. Russian sources put confirmed Soviet losses at only eight tanks and AFVs, but data from the 185th Separate Tank Regiment is not available for 14–15 June. The majority of the Soviet tank losses were suffered by the 185th Separate Tank Regiment which started the battle with 17 T-34 tanks but was down to two tanks on the second day of fighting. The difference, 15 tanks, when added to the eight confirmed losses, matches the final figures.

Finnish StuG III kill claims by type			
T-34	61	T-34-85	4
ISU-152	13	T-70	2
KV-1	5	Unknown	2

The 31st Guards Separate Heavy Breakthrough Tank Regiment, commanded by Major P.D. Primachenko, was in the area at the time and lost seven KV tanks from the start of the offensive to the conclusion of the Kuuterselkä battle. The remains of the 27th Guards Separate Heavy Tank Regiment, commanded by Lieutenant Colonel D.A. Gnezdilov, were also in the area, and lost one IS-2M tank out of five available from the start of the offensive through to the conclusion of the battle. It seems likely that the Soviet heavy-tank losses at Kuuterselkä consisted of one IS-2 and one KV-1. The 1222nd SPG Regiment, commanded by Lieutenant Colonel I.A. Biryukov, reported a total loss of four SU-76M self-propelled guns; a further seven had to be sent for repair. It is likely that destroyed 'assault guns' referred to in Finnish reports have later been misinterpreted to be ISU-152 heavy assault guns when in fact they were SU-76Ms. If any ISU-152s were lost at Kuuterselkä, they presumably came from the 351st Heavy Self-propelled Artillery Regiment, commanded by Major M.F. Olenikov.

Why did the Finnish StuG III have such a favourable exchange ratio against Soviet tanks? According to Finnish claims, the advantage was more than eight-to-one. Kill claims, whether by tanks or fighter aircraft, tend to be exaggerated for a variety of reasons; but even if the Finnish claims are significantly discounted, it does appear that the Finns had a significantly better record of combat success than their Soviet opponents. This advantage was not so much technological as tactical. The StuG III was not significantly better or worse than the T-34 across a wide range of battlefield conditions; and because of the near parity in many technical aspects, battlefield circumstances played a more significant role than any specific technical advantage.

Highest-scoring Finnish StuG III crews			
Vehicle	Kills	Gunner	Commander
Ps. 531-10 'Bubi'	11	Lance Corporal O. Soimala	Staff Sergeant/2nd Lieutenant B. Brotell
Ps. 531-12 'Lea'	9	Lance Corporal M. Kokkonen	Corporal S. Karukka, Sergeant V. Kuusisto
Ps. 531-5 'Amalia'	8	Corporal O. Taponen	Lieutenant O. Aulanko, Corporal I. Koskiniemi*
Ps. 531-8 'Aili'	6	Lance Corporal H. Kauhanen	Lieutenant A. Peltonen**
Ps. 531-9 'Toini'	7	Lance Corporal K. Muona	Lieutenant M. Kiuasperä
Ps. 531-25 'Kyllikki'	7	Armourman S. Vuorela	Sergeant E. Halonen***
Ps. 531-6 'Liisa'	5	Lance Corporal T. Juomoja	Lieutenant O. Aulanko
Ps. 531-7 'Anneli'	5	Lance Corporal L. Leppänen	Sergeant E. Vartia
Ps. 531-14	5	Armourman E. Paakkinen	Sergeant A. Merivirta
*Originally on Ps. 531-6 'Liisa'. **Later on Ps. 531-4 'Lisbeth'. ***Originally on Ps. 531-24.			

US operational research has generally suggested that the dominant factor in tank-vs-tank duels is generally the engagement circumstances. Studies of tank warfare conducted at Johns Hopkins University in the 1950s demonstrated that the side which spotted the enemy and engaged first enjoyed up to a six-fold advantage – in essence, 'see first, engage first, hit first'. This was clearly the case at Kuuterselkä, where Lieutenant Sartio's assault-gun platoon surprised the Soviet T-34s in the initial engagement. From a purely technical point of view, the T-34s should have had the advantage in a close-range duel because of their rotating turrets. Sartio's StuG III was forced to execute a 90-degree turn to confront the Soviet tanks, three of which were destroyed. The surprise factor trumped the technical factors.

Tanks fighting from a defensive position have a clear advantage against enemy armour moving into battle, because the stationary armoured vehicles are more likely to see the advancing enemy first, and then to engage first. The Johns Hopkins University research indicated that tanks defending from well-prepared positions have a 3-to-1 advantage against assaulting tanks. This is sometimes called the 'ambush advantage', because as often as not, the tank or AFV in a stationary defensive position spots the opposing tank first

and hits it before the opposing tank is even aware of the presence of enemy armour. The battle of Kuuterselkä was a meeting engagement in which neither side regularly enjoyed an ambush advantage. However, the performance of the Assault Gun Battalion at the subsequent battle of Tali-Ihantala can probably be attributed to this 'ambush advantage'.

A second vitally important aspect of armoured warfare is the quality of the crews, who must be well enough trained to have a high probability of scoring a hit with the first round fired. After World War II, the Soviet Army conducted studies of the consequences of tank-crew quality during an encounter between equivalent tanks. In situations where two well-trained crews confronted one another, the friendly tank had a 38.4 per cent chance of knocking out the enemy AFV. Conversely, when a highly trained crew faced poorly trained opponents, the likelihood increased to almost 63 per cent. The probability of destroying the enemy tank dropped to less than 4 per cent when two poorly trained crews met in battle. Because data on Soviet tank-crew training in 1944 is largely lacking, however, it is difficult to apply this study to the outcome of the Finnish–Soviet engagements.

Following the battle of Kuuterselkä, the Finnish Sturmi crews adopted the German practice of painting 'kill' rings on the barrels of their assault guns. This is Staff Sergeant Börje Brotell, commander of the highest-scoring Sturmi, photographed on 7 July 1944 while marking his Sturmi, Ps. 531-10 'Bubi'. The crew, including gunner Lance Corporal Olli Soimala, had claimed their seventh kill on 29 June. (SA-kuva)

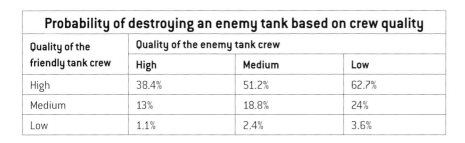

Probability of destroying an enemy tank based on crew quality			
Quality of the friendly tank crew	Quality of the enemy tank crew		
	High	Medium	Low
High	38.4%	51.2%	62.7%
Medium	13%	18.8%	24%
Low	1.1%	2.4%	3.6%

FURTHER READING

One of the Finnish heroes of the battle of Kuuterselkä was Lance Corporal Olof Lagus, age 18, son of Major General Ernst Ruben Lagus, the commander of the Finnish Armoured Division. Lagus was the gunner in Lieutenant Mauri Sartio's Sturmi (Ps. 531-19 'Marjatta') and hit four Soviet T-34 tanks in a few moments in the first clash north of Kuuterselkä. He was wounded on 27 June at Nurmilampi and is shown in hospital with a young nurse before returning to his unit on 14 September 1944. (SA-kuva)

The technical and combat history of the StuG III is well documented in the Muller/ Zimmermann and Laugier books along with a number of other specialized monographs. The National Archives of Finland has the after-action report of the Assault Gun Battalion online on their Digitaaliarkisto site (http://digi.narc.fi/digi/ slistaus.ka?ay=75291). Käkelä's book is a detailed history of the Finnish Assault Gun Battalion and has a detailed account of the battle of Kuuterselkä from the battalion's perspective.

Although there are numerous books and specialized monographs on the T-34 in Russian, there is still no definitive history; the recent Kolomiets books come closest. The fighting at Kuuterselkä is covered in most Russian surveys of the 1944 Finnish campaign, but there are few specialized accounts beyond the Bazuyev article. Two websites were especially valuable in preparing this book: Andreas Larka's blog (http:// www.andreaslarka.net/sturmi.html) provides extensive detail on the Finnish Sturmi; and Peter Samsonov's Tank Archives (http://tankarchives.blogspot.com) provides a wealth of material on Soviet tank development in general and the T-34 in particular, and is especially valuable for the English-speaking readership.

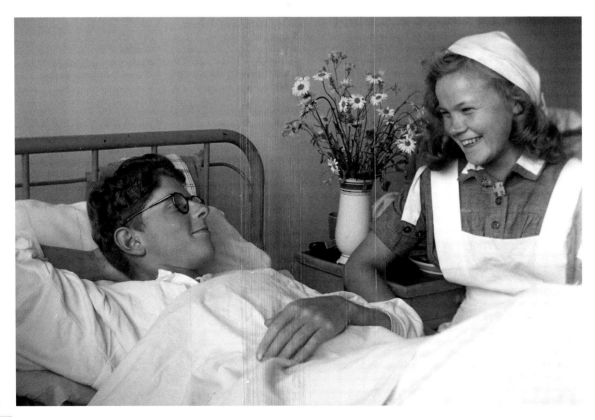

Bazuyev, Denis (2011). 'Vosem geroev za boy', in *Bronya*, No. 2, 2011: 24–27.

Drabkin, Artem & Sheremet, Oleg (2006). *T-34 in Action*. Barnsley: Pen & Sword.

Käkelä, Erkki (1996). *Laguksen rynnäkkötykit: Rynnäkkötykkipataljoona 1943–45*. Helsinki: W. Soderstrom.

Karankevich, L.N. & Kazunenko, D.A. (2017). *Iun 1944 goda: Khronika pervikh dney sovetskogo nastupleniya na Karelskom peresheyke*, St Petersburg: Giol.

Kavalerchik, Boris (2018). *The Tanks of Operation Barbarossa*. Barnsley: Pen & Sword.

Kolomiets, Maksim (2012). *Proslavlenniy T-34*. Moscow: Yauza.

Kolomiets, Maksim (2017). *Sovetskiy sredniy tank T-34*. Moscow: Yauza.

Krivosheyev, G.F., ed. (2010). *Rossiya i SSSR v voynakh XX veka: Kniga poteri*. Moscow: Veche.

Kuusela, Kair (200). *Wehrmachtin panssarit suomessa-Panzers in Finland*. Helsinki: Wiking Divisioona.

Laugier, Didier (2011). *Sturmartillerie*, 2 vols. Saint-Martin-des-Entrées: Heimdal.

Michulec, Robert & Zientarzewski, M. (2007). *T-34: Mythical Weapon*. Mississauga: Air Connection.

Moshchanskiy, Ilya (2006). *Sovetskiy sredniy tank T-34-85: rannie versii zavoda No. 112*. Moscow: Voennaya Letopis.

Muikku, Esa & Purhonnen, Jukka (1997). *Suomalaiset Panssarivaunet 1918–1997*. Helsinki: Apali.

Muller, Peter & Zimmermann, Wolfgang (2009). *Sturmgeschütz III: Development, Production, Deployment*, 2 vols. Andelfingen: History Facts.

Nenye, Vesa, et al. (2016). *Finland at War: The Continuation and Lapland Wars 1941–45*. Oxford: Osprey Publishing.

Polonskiy, V.A., ed. (2005). *Glavnoe avtobronetankovoe upravlenie: Lyudi, sobytiya, fakty v dokumentakh*, 5 vols. Moscow: Defence Ministry of the Russian Federation.

Shirokorad, A.B. (2009). *Tankovaya voyna na vostochnom fronte*. Moscow: Veche.

Solyankin, A.G., et al. (2005). *Otechestvennye bronirovannye mashiny XX vek: Tom 2 1941–45*. Moscow: Eksprint.

Spielberger, Walter (1993). *Sturmgeschütz & Its Variants*. Atglen, PA: Schiffer.

Ustyantsev, Sergey (2010). *Ocherki istorii otechestvennoy industralnoy kultury XX veka, Chast II: Uralskiy tankoviy Zavod No. 183*. Nizhni Tagil: Uralvagon.

Ustyantsev, Sergey, & Kolmakov, D. (2005). *Boevye mashiny uravagonzvoda tank T-34*. Nizhni Tagil: Media-Print.

Vasilyev, Larisa, et al. (2005). *Pravda o tanke T-34*. Moscow: Moskovskie uchebniki.

Yermolov, A. Yu. (2012). *Gosudarstvennoe upravlenie voennoy promyshlennostyu v 1940-e gody: Tankovaya promyshlennost*. St Petersburg: Aleteyya.

INDEX

References to illustrations are shown in **bold**.